PRAISE FOR **ALL FISHERMEN ARE LIARS**

"*All Fishermen Are Liars* is rich in the savvy, humor, and sidelong takes on our sport that have made all of John's books such addictive reading."

—Paul Schullery, author of *If Fish Could Scream*
and *The Fishing Life*

"John Gierach remains the most consistently eloquent fly-fishing writer of modern times."

—James R. Babb, Editor, *Gray's Sporting Journal*

"From the early days . . . to his present cult status, [Gierach's] candor and canniness at the water's edge have been consistent. . . . The voice of the common angler."

—David Profumo, *The Wall Street Journal*

"A reader can learn a whole lot about fishing—and about life—than they might have expected reading this book."

—Kate Whittle, *The Missoula Independent*

"John Gierach is one of the most successful fishing writers of all time, and with good reason. In his 17th book, Gierach reminds us in a delightful way that fishing never has been just about catching, though he can teach us a lot about that, too."

—David Shaffer, *Minneapolis Star Tribune*

"Unfailingly witty, generous of spirit, and full of hard-won but easily shared knowledge. . . . It goes without saying that Gierach is a masterful storyteller, but what's even more obvious after reading *Liars* is that he is a profoundly skilled writer."

—Steve Duda, *The Flyfish Journal*

"A fisherman's testimony to the faithful. . . . [An] elegiac tribute to the elusive art and ineffable pleasure of flyfishing, with plenty of information about how it's done by true practitioners."

—*Kirkus Reviews*

"If you want to fall in love with fly fishing, then Gierach is your man. . . . If you can't be standing knee-deep in a beautiful mountain stream with a fly rod in your hand, then reading a book by Gierach is the next best thing."

—Ed Godfrey, *The Daily Oklahoman*

"[Gierach is] one of the best when it comes to bringing the heart and soul of fly fishing to anglers everywhere. Fly fishermen will find Gierach's latest book to be a great read, while non-anglers will discover the lure of a mountain stream through Gierach's special vision and brand of humor."

—D'Arcy Egan, *The Plain Dealer*

ALL FISHERMEN ARE LIARS

JOHN GIERACH

Art by Glenn Wolff

Simon & Schuster Paperbacks

New York   London   Toronto   Sydney   New Delhi

Simon & Schuster Paperbacks
An Imprint of Simon & Schuster, Inc.
1230 Avenue of the Americas
New York, NY 10020

First Simon & Schuster trade paperback edition April 2015

SIMON & SCHUSTER PAPERBACKS and colophon are registered trademarks
of Simon & Schuster, Inc.

For information about special discounts for bulk purchases,
please contact Simon & Schuster Special Sales at
1-866-506-1949 or business@simonandschuster.com.

The Simon & Schuster Speakers Bureau can bring authors
to your live event. For more information or to book an event,
contact the Simon & Schuster Speakers Bureau at
1-866-248-3049 or visit our website at www.simonspeakers.com.

Designed by Akasha Archer

Manufactured in the United States of America

10 9 8 7

The Library of Congress has cataloged the hardcover edition as follows:

Gierach, John, date.
All fisherman are liars./John Gierach.
—First Simon & Schuster hardcover edition.
      pages   cm
1. Fly fishing—Anecdotes. I. Title.
SH456.G579 2014
799.12'4—dc23   2013012784
ISBN 978-1-4516-1831-0
ISBN 978-1-4516-1832-7 (pbk)
ISBN 978-1-4516-1833-4 (ebook)

All fishermen are liars except you and me
(and sometimes I wonder about you).
—ANONYMOUS

CONTENTS

1

A DAY AT THE OFFICE

Chances are you're raised in the country or in a small town *surrounded* by country: someplace where you can easily walk or ride your bike to the edge of what until recently had been the known world, and then on into the fields, woods and creeks beyond. Some of this is private land and you occasionally have to crawl through a barbed-wire fence to get on it, but the niceties of ownership are left to the adults to sort out. To a kid, it's all just unpopulated and there to explore. The first time a farmer yells at you for trespassing, you honestly don't know what he's talking about.

You're equipped for this wilderness with a hand-me-down folding knife and the Army-issue compass your father brought home from World War Two. The weight of these items in your pocket feels comfortingly substantial; although you understand only in a theoretical way that the compass is some sort of insurance against getting lost. You haven't yet learned the hard lesson that it doesn't matter where north is if you don't know which direction you came from.

In addition to the knife and compass, you have a cane fishing pole with a line stout enough to land a tarpon, as well as a slingshot that seems potentially lethal but maddeningly inaccurate. You also have a crude homemade spear that you keep hidden because you know Dad will ask what you plan to do with it and you won't have an acceptable answer. Taken together, these items constitute the beginning of a lifelong fascination with the tools of sport.

You experience the kind of freedom that will be unknown to future generations. This is the 1950s, when kids are still allowed to run wild as long as they're home by dark. It's also a time when low-grade delinquency—like trespassing, truancy or the odd fistfight—comes under the heading of "boys will be boys." You might get scolded or spanked, but you won't have to undergo counseling.

Like all children, you take your play as seriously as any young predator. The only difference you see when you begin to tag along with the grown-ups on actual hunting and fishing trips is that their toys are larger, heavier and in some cases louder than yours. At first you're there as a mascot, unable to keep up and making too much noise, but eventually you see that this is serious adult business and prove yourself enough to trade the slingshot for a .22 rifle and graduate to a rod with a reel on it.

Dad begins to sense an opportunity. When the time comes for you to have your own shotgun, he gives you the Fox Sterlingworth

12-gauge he got from your grandfather. (It's a little more gun than you can handle, but you'll grow into it.) Then he acts surprised to find that he no longer has a shotgun and says he guesses he'll just have to buy himself a new one. It turns out to be the sexy Italian double he's been mooning over for years. The same thing happens with other gear until, by your late teens, Dad has all new stuff and your room looks like a used sporting goods store.

Hunting and fishing are the two things you and your father can always talk about easily, but over time other subjects become quagmires. There's the competition over the family sedan that comes with the first driver's license; the first serious awareness of politics spurred by the civil rights movement and the assassination of President Kennedy; books that weren't assigned at school and that some of your teachers disapprove of; loud rock and roll and a certain dark-haired girl with big, soft eyes. In hindsight, you think you must have been confused, but at the time, you seem pretty damned sure of yourself.

By the time you head off to college, you've begun to drift away from sport and are now trying to picture yourself as a poet and intellectual. On the other hand, you bring along your .22 and take the occasional break in season for some rabbit hunting. You now understand what trespassing is, and this time when the farmer yells at you, you explain that you're a struggling college student just trying to get a cottontail for dinner, exaggerating the poverty angle a little, but not exactly lying. He takes in the long hair and the attempt at a beard. Then he says, "Next time, stop by the house first."

You've also brought a rod and there's a slow, brown river flowing through town, but you've never seen anyone fishing it and can't imagine anything living in water with that peculiar industrial aroma. It's only years later that you wonder what you'd have found if you'd followed the thing upstream, past the outflow from the brewery and on into farm country. But at the time, you're too busy with books, lectures, political demonstrations, music, beer, early struggles with writing and another girl with big eyes. She's your third. Or maybe fourth.

After graduation you're offered a job in the bar you've been drinking in for the last four years. You suspect this is an act of charity. Your major was philosophy, which the bar owner has described as "a quaint but useless discipline." With your bachelor's degree in hand and no plans for graduate school, you begin to see his point.

This tavern has seemed more like home than your various apartments and trailers, but you're envisioning a bigger change than switching from one side of the bar to the other. You're unemployed if not actually unemployable and have no other prospects, so you drive out to the Rocky Mountains to look around.

In Colorado, in a town at an elevation of 10,000 feet with five year-round residents (how did you end up here?), you go to work in a silver mine for room, board and shares. You're living in a cabin on the mine property with two other young guys at loose ends: an out-of-work actor and a sullen revolutionary type who reveals nothing whatsoever about his past, including his last name. It's possible that he just values his privacy, but you suspect he's on the lam.

The room is okay, but the board is on the thin side, tending toward beans and tortillas, so you rediscover fishing, this time for trout. They seem small—on the order of bluegills—but they're the loveliest fish you've ever seen and they live in country where both the scenery and the altitude take your breath away—one figuratively, the other literally.

You don't have much money, but you buy a fly rod and later a rifle for mule deer. You had a deer rifle of sorts when you came west, but somewhere along the line you traded it for a used fuel pump and a tank of gas. It was a surplus .303 Enfield. No great loss.

The Second World War has been over for twenty-five years now, but the used equipment is still readily available and cheap, so it constitutes most of your outdoor gear: clothing, packs, pup tents, sleeping bags, tarps, sheath knives, canteens, mess kits, Dad's old compass and so on. If our troops in that conflict had been issued fly rods, you'd have one of those, too.

In the end, the shares in the mine you've been counting on don't pan out. It turns out that the owner sold several hundred percent of the thing to gullible investors and it's largely worthless anyway. Eventually the authorities get involved.

But no one comes to evict you from the cabin and you realize you could squat there indefinitely. It's tempting. There's firewood to cut, water to haul, fish and game in the surrounding mountains and some blue-collar fun to be had in a tavern twenty miles down a dirt road. On the other hand, you're broke, there's no work and you'd freeze over the winter, so you and your partners drift off in different directions. You never see either of them again.

There's a side trip to New York City, where you stay with a girl-friend from college, work a low-paying job and try to be a writer. None of it works out and one day you inadvertently panhandle a friend from college. You don't recognize him at first because he's wearing a sport coat and has cut his hair short. He buys you lunch and slips you a twenty. You're embarrassed, but you eat the cheese-burger and take the money.

Not long after that you go back to Colorado. You tell yourself you weren't defeated by the city, it's just that you couldn't stop thinking about mountains and rivers and brightly colored trout swimming in cold, clean water.

You find a cheap place to live, trade your car for a seriously used four-wheel-drive and register it in Colorado so you can buy resident fishing and hunting licenses. You begin a series of manual-labor jobs to get by. You're young and strong and a good worker, but your mind habitually wanders to the fishing and writing you now do in every minute of your time off. One day a boss catches you daydreaming and says, "You know, another hump like you comes down the pike every day." You reply, "Yeah, and there's another shitty job like this one around every corner." It's becoming clear that you don't have a future in the diplomatic service. In fact, you're not at all sure what you have in mind for yourself, but it's beginning to look like it might involve a typewriter instead of a shovel.

You marry one of the girls with big, dark eyes, but it doesn't last. When the justice of the peace who tied the knot asked if you'd thought this through, you said, "Sure," but in fact you hadn't. The divorce is painless. She doesn't want the books, the rifle or the fly rod. You have no use for the herbal tea, the tarot cards or the teepee.

Other women in your life also work out temporarily, but eventually they all begin to give you a certain quizzical look that you come to recognize. They're asking themselves, "What was I thinking?"

You continue to try things on for size: jobs, friends, ideas, writing styles, outdoor sports, various controlled substances that are available at the time and a wide range of wild country in all seasons. You realize that you can't write what you know when you don't know anything, so you travel compulsively and try everything. You make some mistakes, but none of them are fatal, although you do injure a knee, frostbite some toes and bugger an elbow, and none of them are ever quite the same again.

In a college town you meet some writers and some fly fishers and settle in to learn the respective crafts. You've been writing since high school and fishing since before you can remember, but it turns out you know less about either than you thought you did. On the other hand, you're not entirely surprised to find that success in both disciplines depends on patience, persistence, diligence and attention to detail. These were never your strong points, but you vow to change.

You publish here and there in literary magazines for bragging rights, but no money. You even get a thin volume of poems into print, but come to see that poetry is unlikely to dollar up, as they say out

West. As someone once said, "A publisher would rather see a burglar in his office than a poet."

You also manage to catch some trout.

In the grand scheme of things, these are not enormous accomplishments, but they make you inordinately happy. Decades later you review your Social Security earnings record and find that several of those years are commemorated by columns of zeros. You wonder how you managed to keep body and soul together. Apparently you were destitute, but that's not how you remember it.

You live in an odd succession of houses and apartments with an equally odd succession of people: students, former students, would-be students, struggling writers, painters, musicians, craftsmen and others who defy categorization. You attend periodic house meetings to determine the identity of the people on the floor in sleeping bags. If no one who's paying rent knows them, they're asked to leave.

You're neither a great writer nor a great fisherman, but these continue to be the two things you care about most and it's a surprisingly long time before it occurs to you to put the two together. Finally you write a story about fly fishing and sell it to a magazine for the equivalent of a month's wages. This is the first time you've been paid actual money for something you've written. The now-comfortable role of starving artist notwithstanding, it feels pretty damned good.

You begin to freelance for fishing magazines, go to work as the outdoor columnist for a daily newspaper and publish a book that does well enough for the publisher to ask if you have another one in the works. It just so happens that you do. It's a gradual start, but when fly fishing begins to get fashionable, you're already in place: maybe not a top gun, but a somewhat established writer just the same. This is the equivalent of pulling off at a random turnout along an unknown river, stumbling into the cosmic green drake hatch and having the right fly.

The books, the magazines and the newspaper don't pay all that well individually, but taken together they sometimes add up to enough. It happens slowly, with several false starts, but finally you quit the last of an interminable series of part-time jobs and begin making a living as a writer.

This leads to occasional misunderstandings. Some people assume that you're now rich because the only other writer they know anything about is Ernest Hemingway. These include some who should know better, like the guy who writes in the London *Times* that your populist persona is just an act and that you're actually an eccentric millionaire. What? Luckily, none of your friends read the London *Times,* but they do read the magazine that names you "angler of the year." You're delighted, but the ribbing is unmerciful, beginning with the friend who asks, "So, have those guys ever *fished* with you?"

You meet a man who, in the course of a durable friendship, teaches you most of what you'll ever know about fly fishing and incidentally helps you dial yourself back in the direction of the native midwesterner you'd always been. He's also what you'd call "colorful," so you naturally write about him and early on people ask if he's real, or just a fictional character. Years later, when he goes on the road as a public speaker and you become somewhat reclusive, people ask him the same thing about you.

You buy a small, mediocre house near a small, mediocre trout stream, and after a few good years you manage to pay off the mortgage. This leaves you nearly broke, but you own your home outright, which is crucial for a writer—a profession in which the regular paychecks needed for monthly payments are all but unknown.

You grow a decent garden in black, river-bottom soil, raise chickens for eggs, meat and hackle, heat with wood you cut yourself, and hunt, fish and forage for at least some of the groceries. You learn, among other things, that as satisfying as subsistence is, it's a full-time job that will be hard to maintain. The garden goes first. You've begun to travel a lot during the growing season, and the hippie girl next door who agrees to weed and water it for a share of the harvest sometimes gets distracted and forgets.

You meet another girl with those big, dark eyes you could never resist. Woman, actually. It's been a while now since either of you were kids. She's a writer herself and comes from a long line of Great Lakes fishermen, so those are two things you don't have to explain. You've been a couple for some time when she heads back to Michigan to fish with her family. When you drop her off at the airport, you jokingly say, "Catch a fish for me." When you pick her up a week later, a crate large enough to hold a railroad tie rolls onto the baggage carousel. She says, "There's your fish." It's a thirty-pound Chinook salmon. By this time you've moved in together. There wasn't much discussion. It just sort of happened. It also just sort of happens that twenty-some years later you're still together.

You live within driving distance of some of the best trout fishing in the country and there's an airport an hour and a half away, so you see a lot of rivers, streams and lakes, sometimes on assignment, sometimes on your own dime. These waters are all beautiful in their own way, but in the course of your travels you discover a few real sweet spots: places that are incomparable and unforgettable for reasons that usually have to do with the fishing, as well as something else that you glimpse from time to time, but that resists being distilled into sentences and paragraphs. You want to believe that at least some of these places are remote enough to adequately protect themselves, but then time and experience reveal that to be less true than you'd hoped.

So in your stories you begin to casually omit the name of a stream or river, or change its name, or move its location from one state or province to another in order to protect the innocent. You don't really think you can single-handedly hold off the inevitable, but you do hope you can keep it from being your fault.

In extreme cases, you engage in the fantasy that certain places don't exist and even if they do, you were never there. The transaction between writer and reader comes with some responsibility, but if you never write the story, all bets are off. You realize you've become one of those people who make a living with public words, and although you're not in the same class with lawyers and politicians, one thing you share with them is the real possibility of doing more harm than good. You adopt a quote from novelist Thomas McGuane as your professional motto: "Whenever you feel like falling silent, do it."

There was no calculation in this, but over time you develop a reputation in some circles as the rare fishing writer who can and will keep his mouth shut and are therefore sometimes taken to secret glory holes that few ever get to see. The worst that happens is that you occasionally go fishing without turning a profit: something normal people do every day.

You're now and then implicated as part of the fly-fishing industry. You don't quite see it that way, but denying it seems pointless, so you take to saying, "I don't do this because it's a business; it's a business so I can do this." You also begin quoting John Mellencamp, who said, "I never cared about money—but I always wanted to get paid."

It's a passable living and a good life. You have all the usual troubles—financial, medical, personal—plus a few that are peculiar to your profession, but you're doing the only two things you ever really wanted to do. You're profoundly interested in fishing when you're fishing and just as fascinated by writing when you're at your desk. Both are great fun when they're going well, and still worth the effort even when they're not. When an interviewer asks if you consider yourself a fisherman first and a writer second or vice versa, you truthfully answer, "Yes."

You may not have actually beaten the system, but there are certain small victories. For instance, the accountant who now handles your taxes says that if some of his other self-employed clients saw what you legitimately write off—fly rods, travel, fishing lodges, guide tips, etc.—they'd "shit a brick." You now pay more in taxes in a year than you used to make as a writer. You suppose that amounts to prog-ress.

Some days this seems like such an uncertain career that you wonder if you should have done something else. Other days you have so much fun you can't believe you're actually getting paid. Finally it occurs to you that you've pretty much accomplished everything you set out to do, it's just that you didn't set out to do all that much. You realize that you've been writing about fly fishing professionally for thirty-five years and still haven't run out of things to say. This can mean only one of two things: that the subject itself is inexhaustible or that you'll never quite get it right.

There are inevitable complications, but at its core, life is simple. At the desk it's all about the luscious sense, sound and possibilities of language. On the water it's all about the fish and the beautiful places they live. The only real difficulties you encounter are in getting from one place to the other.

In the end, you fish as much as you want to and sometimes even a little more. You begin telling people, "I have to go fishing; it's my job." You don't exactly mean that as a joke, but understand that's how they'll take it. Still, even on those rare days when you trudge off to a trout stream not so much because you want to, but because your live-lihood depends on it, you have a better day at the office than most.

2

GREAT BEAR

It's sometime around midday and either Martin or I—I forget which—have just landed the five-pound lake trout that will be our lunch fish. Our guide, Craig Blackie, motors us to shore, digs out a blackened iron grate and props it off the ground on rocks while Martin and I hunt for firewood. We're at the northern end of Great Bear Lake in Canada's Northwest Territories, above the Arctic Circle and near the northern tree line, so wood is scarce, but we need only enough for a quick twig fire.

By the time Martin and I get back with our meager armloads of willow, Craig has the fish cleaned, slathered in seasoned olive oil and wrapped tightly in tin foil. Two herring gulls are down the shore picking at the guts. The three of us are dressed in wind pants, slickers and hats with earflaps. Craig is wearing fingerless gloves that his mother knitted out of musk ox wool. It's the third week of August.

We stand there talking shop in the way of men who don't know each other well, but are comfortable together. Martin is a Scot who's fished extensively in Europe and North America. Craig is studying for a doctoral degree in fisheries biology with a specialty in lake trout and is the most knowledgeable guide I've ever met. I contribute what I can.

We're in a starkly beautiful arctic landscape that not everyone gets to see, but instead of rubbernecking we gaze at steam escaping from the foil-wrapped fish while open cans of pork and beans and stewed tomatoes begin to bubble around the edges. The fishing here is good enough that no one even thought about bringing a backup lunch of sandwiches.

Size can exert a kind of tyranny in fishing. As a lifelong trout fisherman, I refuse to think of our lunch fish as "little" when it's about to feed three grown men and only half an hour earlier was pulling 8-weight line off a reel. On the other hand, in the hour before lunchtime we'd gone through at least a dozen bigger lake trout looking for one small enough to eat.

My first and biggest fish that day wasn't exactly an accident, but I can't say I was ready for it. On the way out to a submerged rock bar to troll, we'd passed a small cove that Craig said could be good for grayling, and he asked if we wanted to rig up some lighter rods and try it. I've always had a soft spot for grayling, and Martin is a past president of the Grayling Society, so it wasn't a hard sell.

We'd been casting from shore for about twenty minutes without a take when Craig walked over and said, "Let's give it a few more minutes and then move." (Grayling are usually easy enough to catch, but they're not always where they're supposed to be.) Right about then a large, grayish-green shape swam casually over to my fly and stopped. To Craig's eternal credit, he didn't yell, "Set!" but let me sink the hook myself. I was fishing a rig that was appropriate for grayling of maybe four pounds tops—a 5-weight rod with a size 8 Muddler Minnow on a 5x tippet—and this fish looked like it could be a yard long.

Craig said, "I'll go get the boat."

Once we were able to follow the fish, the situation didn't seem quite so desperate, although I never got past wishing I'd hooked this thing on heavier tackle, and the end game at the net—where fish are often lost—was especially ticklish. It was a lake trout that weighed just a hair over seventeen pounds—almost four times the breaking strength of my tippet. It was handsome and healthy-looking, but it didn't have the distended gut you sometimes see, meaning he probably hadn't had his breakfast yet.

That could explain why a fish of that size was interested in my little size 8 streamer, which would normally be too small a fly for lake trout. Craig told me later that one of these fish could eat a quarter of its body weight at a single sitting, so that if the cove had been full of grayling that morning, it might have weighed more like twenty-two pounds. On the other hand, if the fish hadn't been so hungry, I probably wouldn't have caught him.

Except for that one, we got all our lake trout that day by trolling. This is the preferred method on these big northern lakes simply because it's so efficient. It's not that you couldn't cast to any of the places you'd troll through—you're usually fishing at a depth of less than twenty feet—but to cover anything close to the same amount of water by casting and retrieving a big fly on a sinking line, you'd have to put in eighteen-hour days and ice your elbow every night.

As usual, there's what we like to think of as a science to it, but the key isn't so much how or what you troll as where. You're looking for submerged points, steep drop-offs and open-water rock bars that attract smaller organisms—from midge and caddis larvae to ciscoes and sticklebacks to grayling—and the bigger predators that follow them. But of course *you're* not looking for them because your guide knows exactly where they are, as well as which ones are fishier than others, depending on the conditions. He's done this for thousands of hours and motors right to them, even the ones that lie in what appears to be featureless open water.

I was using an 8-weight rod and a line with interchangeable sink tips that allow you to vary your depth. I'd pay out almost the entire fly line and take up a short shock loop held as lightly as possible between the reel and the index finger of my rod hand. The idea here is that the fish pulls the loop straight when he hits, giving him time to turn and take the hook in the corner of his jaw. A fish that hits while you're trolling can feel like it's hooked itself, but there's a lot of stretch in all that line, so you want to reef hard on the set to make sure. Of course every fish you hook takes you into the backing, but when you have only four turns of line left on your arbor, that's not always as impressive as it sounds.

I did well with simple, three-or-four-inch-long rabbit fur streamers tied on 3/0 salmon hooks or as tube flies. Good colors were pink and white, blue and white, and all white with a flash of red. Some lake trout fishermen apply the big-fish, big-fly theory and use tandem hook trolling streamers that can be a foot long. These are fine for dragging behind a boat—where they feel like you've hooked a small trout—but they're ungainly for any other use, although in a pinch they *are* castable in a clunky, duck-on-the-forward-cast kind of way.

There are those of us who love this kind of esoteric tackle fiddling for the illusion of mastery it gives us. We can go on about it long enough to bore even another fisherman, but the truth is, trolling isn't rocket science. Some fly fishers say they don't care for it for just that reason: because it seems too haphazard and, God forbid, unskilled. Maybe it is, but only in the way of any other style of fly fishing designed to systematically cover fishy-looking water. I don't really see a tactical difference between trolling for lake trout and methodically swinging a wet fly down a likely-looking pool that may or may not hold an Atlantic salmon. Both have the same hypnotic quality that allows your mind to wander, only to be periodically wrenched back to the present in no uncertain terms. If I were one to offer advice on trolling to other fly fishers, I'd say the same thing their mothers said about spinach: At least try it before you say you don't like it.

For that matter, I've met any number of fly fishermen who can't get excited about catching lake trout, although it isn't clear why. I've heard it said that they don't fight well, but in my experience, at much past eight or ten pounds they're a real handful on a fly rod, and they go way past that. Lake trout are the largest of the char—the same family that includes the beloved brook trout. They readily take flies, and under the right conditions they can grow as big as tarpon. A constant reminder of that at Great Bear Lake is that at six feet and 160 pounds, *I* would fit in any of the big nets the guides carry. But I guess there's no accounting for taste.

That night at dinner I located my name tag and sat down with some guys from Winnipeg who'd had a good day trolling with spoons. They do put name tags on the dinner tables, which struck me as quaintly formal, and I couldn't help wondering how they decided who should sit with whom. My best guess is that since there were both fly and gear fishermen in camp—not to mention the odd switch-hitter—this was simply an attempt to keep us from huddling with our own kind out of habit.

These dinners were crowded and boisterous and could be disorienting after a quiet day on the water. There were twenty-five fishermen in camp that week and that many people eating and bragging at once can raise the decibel level. And this against a backdrop of nearly that many more waitresses, cooks, guides, pilots, mechanics and others who seemed constantly busy, even though you couldn't always guess at their job descriptions. One especially cold, wet day when we were fishing close to camp, we came in to get warm and have lunch out of the rain. A man down at the dock told me, "If you go in the back door of the kitchen, the woman there will give you a big, wet kiss and a hot lunch, or, if you're lucky, just lunch." On his tax return, this guy's occupation would be listed as "camp comedian."

But even with all those fishermen in camp, it was rare to see another boat on the water, and when you did, it wasn't much more than a speck passing in the distance, too far away to hear the outboard. That was no accident. Great Bear Lake is an inland sea covering just over twelve thousand square miles, and although you can reach only a corner of it by boat from the lodge, there's still a lot of water to spread out in. The guides are also fully aware that no one wants to fly all that way into the Canadian wilderness to fish in a crowd, so every evening they divvy up first, second and third choices so no one gets in anyone else's hair. These meetings sometimes delve into the fishermen's skill levels and the amount of babysitting they require and so are best held in private. That's one reason why the guides don't sit down to dinner with the clients. Another is that, however charming we might be, after eight or ten hours with us, they could stand a break.

Unless a guide has made arrangements with one of the clients to go out and fish in the evening, he's likely to finish his dinner and retire to the collection of staff cabins set off at some distance from the rest of the place. This area is known as Guide Land and is strictly off limits to civilians.

Plummer's Great Bear Lake Lodge is one of three established camps and several other fly-outs run by the same outfit. It was founded by Chummy Plummer (the grandfather and namesake of the present owner) and his son Warren in the early 1950s—when life and fishing were both simpler—and by now it sprawls all over a narrow peninsula in Great Bear Lake like the improvised village it is. The place isn't junky, but it was built for function instead of fanciness and does show the inevitable signs of hard human use and nearly sixty brutal Arctic winters. This is more of a comfortably lived-in outpost than a resort: a place where serious fishermen come to fish. Beyond that, all they need or want is a warm, dry place to sleep, three meals a day, a good guide and good fishing, all of which they get. I felt supremely at home here, with no worries about using the wrong fork at dinner. I started fishing in the Midwest at about the time this camp was established, and it still startles me to think that any kind of fishing is considered upscale.

I got my shot at grayling a few days later when I did a fly-out to the source of the Horton River with an Australian named Frank. It seems that Frank had gotten it into his head to try for a world record lake trout on two-pound tippet and this was a good place for the attempt. In the fall—and August is fall here—hundreds of grayling work upriver toward the outlet at Horton Lake to feed, while large lake trout prowl down into the gathering current to ambush them. It was understood that Frank and our guide, Mike, would make a serious try for a big lake trout on light tackle at the outlet while I'd have a seat on the float plane and an entire Arctic grayling river all to myself.

The Horton is a typical tundra river: cold, clear, broad and shallow, with placid, but braided currents and a view to the horizon in every direction without a tree in sight. When five big bull caribou wandered over to the river to drink, I could see them coming for a thousand yards: just their antlers at first, which at that distance looked like bentwood rockers bobbing in the middle distance.

The outlet itself was wide, smooth, dish-shaped and pewter-colored under a low, drizzly overcast. The current was nearly imperceptible, but now and then there'd be a large, violent boil followed instantaneously by twenty or thirty smaller boils as a good-sized lake trout lunged into a pod of grayling. Before the day was out, a ten-pound lake trout would be landed with the tail of a two-pound grayling still sticking out of his mouth. When his face was pointed at the camera for a photo, he swallowed defiantly, as if to say "You got me, but you're not gettin' my lunch." A philosophical discussion ensued over whether this was ten pounds of one fish and two pounds of another, or one twelve-pound lake trout, but Mike, using flawless guide logic, declared, "The fish weighs what the scale says it does."

I watched Frank for a few minutes, trying to figure out how he was getting a passably pretty cast out of a rod, line and leader far too light for the big fly he was using. Then I strolled down the river. There were no rises, so I tied on a size 14 soft hackle as a search pattern and got a two-and-a-half-pound grayling on my first swing. It jumped once, made a decent run—scattering the wakes of other fish—and then jumped again before it started to tire. The next three or four grayling were all around two pounds, and then I hooked a fat male with an outlandish dorsal fin that was closer to three. He ran farther and scattered more wakes. I hadn't yet taken a step or made a cast longer than twenty feet.

If I had to guess how many grayling I landed over the next few hours, I'd say it was in the neighborhood of fifty, with a combined weight of something like 125 pounds, and the phrase "shooting fish in a barrel" stuck in my mind like an annoying song. So I quit. I wasn't bored, but there's a point—different for everyone, I suppose—when you have simply caught too many fish too easily and are in danger of not only missing the point, but also of abusing the very thing you claim to love and came so far to see. I've been fishing long enough to have a few memories of big, easy hauls that are tinged with shame. I didn't want this to be one of them.

I found Mike a few hundred yards upstream squatting on the bank cleaning the regulation five-pound lake trout for lunch. "You want a grayling to go with this?" he asked, pointing at the fish with his fillet knife. I said, "Sure," stepped back into the river and had a two-pound fish on my first cast. In this part of the world, backcountry travelers refer to grayling as "river hotdogs." "If there's nothing else to eat," they say, "you can always catch a grayling."

Frank hadn't landed his record fish. He'd hooked a large lake trout on two-pound tippet that would have qualified, but after he played it carefully for over an hour, it threw the hook. He seemed more amused than disappointed. A record fish would have been fun, but he wasn't about to let it ruin even a single morning, let alone the whole trip. The fire was cozy and smoky and the air was redolent with the aroma of cooking fish and beans. Frank looked around and said, "It's beautiful here, isn't it?"

After lunch I offered to go back downriver to stay out of his way. I thought I'd explore a little, look for more wildlife and maybe see if I could get a grayling to take a dry fly, just to mix things up. But Frank said he'd taken his shot and now he was just fishing. "String up your 8-weight and catch some of these lake trout," he said. So I did.

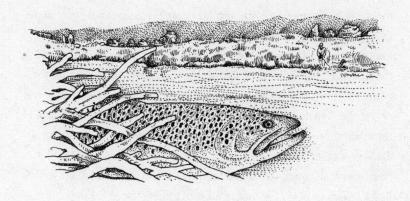

3

K BAR T

As I was driving west across Colorado on Interstate 70, there was a specific quarter mile where the public radio and classic rock stations I'd been grazing through all faded to static and were replaced by country and western, and preachers. The exit for the town of Silt was in the rearview mirror and the Colorado River was off my left shoulder. I'd crossed the Continental Divide some ninety miles back and could have made the Utah border in an hour, but it was only then that I felt like I was officially on the West Slope, where the airwaves are filled with pain and redemption plus livestock reports on the hour.

This was one of those rare times when I'd allowed myself to get too busy for someone with my lazy temperament and was consequently feeling a little sorry for myself. I'd just gotten back from a long trip to northern Canada and had spent days mowing through the mail, messages, bills and chores that had accumulated while I was gone: the boring adult obligations that are all important in one way or another but that add up to drudgery when there are too many of them at one time. In two more days I was supposed to be at the Fly Tackle Retailer Show in Denver, where I had what I'll describe as "business," although to an independent observer it would just look like a bunch of people standing around talking about fishing.

I know, it doesn't sound that bad (you're probably busier than that on your average weekend), but for most of the year I live the kind of slow-paced sporting life where being rushed means not having enough time to loaf between fishing trips.

In the meantime, my friends Mark Weaver and Buzz Cox had invited me to come over and fish with them on the K bar T, a small fly-fishing guest ranch they operate on the White River near the town of Meeker. The scheduling could have been easier-going for my taste. I had a scant two days with a five-and-a-half-hour drive each way, leaving barely more fishing than driving time, but these were the only two days for weeks in either direction when they weren't booked with paying fishermen and could accommodate a freeloading friend.

I'd heard a lot about the place, mostly from Mark. They had a refurbished hundred-plus-year-old ranch house, two miles of the White River, a mile of spring creek and maybe half a mile of a small freestone stream flowing across a hay meadow. The place could handle as many as eight fishermen at a time, although they were more likely to have between two and four, which sounded like a more reasonable number, even if it cut into the bottom line. I was eager to see it and I think Mark and Buzz were just as eager to do a little fishing themselves. Contrary to what some think, guides and outfitters don't get to fish that much. Instead, they're busy doing the countless, mundane, mostly invisible things that allow their *clients* to fish.

I'd never fished the White before. I'd heard it was a good trout river but that most of it was private and what public water there was could be hard to find unless you were a local who was already dialed in. Of course, it's in the nature of rivers like this to be private, at least here in Colorado, with our unenlightened stream access laws. Much of the state is a beautiful but steep, infertile landscape and back in the homesteading days the first settlers grabbed up the river valleys with their flat meadows and year-round water. Desirable real estate being what it is, most of it has stayed in private hands ever since. There was a time when you might have been able to sweet-talk your way onto places like this with a six-pack of beer and the promise of a limit of cleaned trout. Ranchers were often proud of their fishing, but they seldom had time left at the end of a long, hard day to fish it themselves, so it was mostly appreciated by visiting relatives, friends from town and the occasional polite stranger.

You can still wangle access from time to time, but many of these places have now been leased to outfitters to help pay the property taxes or sold outright by people who saw the family spread less as a heritage and more as a grubstake to a different life. The consequence is that some of these places are now fished much harder than they once were and by a different class of people: in extreme cases, those who think roughing it is wearing an L.L. Bean sport coat instead of the usual Louis Vuitton.

I got off the interstate at the town of Rifle, gassed up, grabbed a cup of convenience-store coffee and headed the forty-some miles north on State Highway 13 toward Meeker. The speed limit is sixty, but this is the kind of lonesome two-lane blacktop where you stand an equal chance of being passed by a young buck doing eighty in a dual axle pickup or getting stuck behind an elderly rancher going eighteen miles an hour in a thirty-year-old station wagon. It also pays to keep an eye peeled for cattle. Over here the yellow signs along the shoulder still say OPEN RANGE, while on the east side of the Rockies too many people didn't know what that meant, so they changed them to CAUTION, COWS ON ROAD.

I mention the drive in some detail because the journey itself is the destination, as the Buddhists say, and because it was somewhere up this road that I stopped feeling pressed for time and was suddenly just going fishing. Of course, going fishing always seems like the answer, even when it's not clear what the question was.

I got to the K bar T a little after eleven o'clock and was greeted by Princeton, who passes as the ranch dog. Princeton is the result of a romance between a Chihuahua and something small, white and wiry. He's a friendly little guy with a head smaller than the average house cat and he's smart enough not to venture out into the open where he could be picked off by a golden eagle or red-tailed hawk by day or an owl at night. Given time and an overriding affection for all dogs, you get used to him and remind yourself it's not his fault that he looks like a wet chicken.

After a quick, early lunch, Mark and I drove half a mile across a meadow and waded up a shallow side channel to the river. (Buzz had unspecified ranch business to take care of and said he'd try to join us later.) Here in its upper valley the White is what a Coloradan would call a medium-sized river. It was the second week of September, so it was low enough to be a little bony, but you still had to search out a place shallow enough if you wanted to cross. Mark said it wasn't float-able this high on the drainage except maybe at the height of spring runoff when it would be pointless to fish it.

The ranch is at an elevation of a little over 6,000 feet—almost exactly the same as my place on the other side of the mountains—so I knew that by the end of the month there'd be a hard frost, a glaze of morning bank ice along the river and maybe a dusting of snow. But for now it was still hot, windless high summer: the kind of indolent weather that makes you think of a lawn chair in the shade and a good book. Mark said the last group they'd had in had landed over three hundred trout from this stretch of the White in two days. That's a good testimonial, but it also meant that most if not all of the willing trout there had felt a hook recently and no doubt still remembered it.

Mark left me at a deep, complicated bend pool with an overhanging cottonwood on the far bank and walked upstream to the next run. I ran a size 12 hopper through several current seams and finally got a fourteen-inch brown trout. Then I made a long cast with a hard upstream mend to the shady slick on the far bank. Three things happened simultaneously: I saw that I was at the wrong angle for a good drift, a large trout turned downstream after the fly and the fly itself began to drag enough to leave a wake. Naturally, the fish smelled a rat and disappeared. Chances are he'd had an unpleasant run-in with a grasshopper in the recent past. I waded upstream and made a dozen more casts with better drifts, but the fish was spooked and wasn't about to take a second look.

The rest of the day went very much like that. We started at the top end of the ranch property and leap-frogged downstream, cherry-picking the best-looking runs. This was beautiful water with long, cool, oxygenating riffles pouring into deep, fishy pools, glides and cut banks. But as good as it looked, strikes were scarce and what at first looked like good takes were often large trout turning away at the last possible second, splashing the fly with their tails. Buzz joined us for a few hours in the middle of the afternoon and landed the biggest trout that was caught: a fat cutbow I'll guess at seventeen inches. But for the most part, the fish seemed reticent and spooky, and even those that were tempted usually thought better of it in the end.

I tried a weighted nymph dropper behind my grasshopper, but it didn't help. Neither did swinging a Muddler Minnow. Fishing a brace of nymphs with weight in the deeper runs got us whitefish. Some of them were nice and big and plenty of fun to catch; they just weren't what we were after. The few trout we did get were the smaller ones, at least compared to the dripping hogs in the snapshots at the ranch.

There's an entire school of fly-fishing literature dedicated to techniques for catching trout under difficult conditions. None of it is wrong, but much of it ignores the obvious fact that even the best rivers have their off days, just as even the finest musicians have those nights when they'd rather be home watching *I Love Lucy* reruns than playing another gig. The truth of the matter was put succinctly by the hundred-year-old Michigan angler Rosalynde Johnstone, who once said, "Any fish will bite if the fish are bitin'." Taken either literally or metaphorically, that may be all you need to know.

Buzz left after a while to do more unspecified work. Mark and I fished until dusk, hoping for an evening caddis hatch, but nothing much happened. As hot as it had been during the day, the air chilled quickly when the sun got low, and there weren't many bugs. Mark seemed a little disappointed, as guides often are when what they know to be good water doesn't fish as well as it could. I wouldn't have minded hooking one or two of those big trout that refused my fly, but mostly I was just glad it was me fishing instead of a paying customer who might not have felt he was getting his money's worth. Those high-score days the trout counters are after do happen from time to time, but it's easy to forget that they have lasting if not permanent effects. By all rights, a stretch of water like this should be rested for a week after a three-hundred-fish pounding.

That night Buzz's wife, Rose, fried several chickens with rice and gravy, green beans, coleslaw and cornbread. Rose does the cooking at the K bar T—as she did at High Lonesome Ranch, another fishing outfit south of there where I'd first met these folks—and she's real good at it. Food is important to fishermen. Success, failure and the infinite gradations in between all make us ravenous, and bruised egos at the end of slow days respond especially well to good cooking.

Every outfitter knows that there are people who use a fishing trip as an excuse to do things they'd never think of doing at home. The most manageable of us simply eat too much and fall asleep.

Buzz was quiet at dinner, but then he's always quiet. He's a large taciturn man with the physique of the movie version of a Navy Seal: a large neck, barrel chest and arms so muscular he can't quite drop them to his sides. Even when he's relaxed, he looks like he's about to lift something heavy. He grew up in family fishing camps, got it in his blood and has guided himself for the last twenty years. Rose told me that when he announced a few years ago that they'd be running a lodge—effectively going into what's now called the "hospitality business"—she had her doubts. But as it turned out, Buzz's unthreatening but imposing presence and minimalist conversational style make him a more effective camp manager than the usual talkative glad-hander.

The next morning Buzz, Mark and I drove over to the spring creek, piled into a four-seat ATV and motored up to the top end on a narrow two-track through thick willows. Like all the water on the ranch, this creek is unimproved: basically a mile of willowy marsh with beaver ponds and channels running through it. The springs run all year, but they gush in the spring and dribble in the fall in response to the river-fed water table. This late in the season the water was low and the current imperceptible. It was pleasantly cool early in the day, but the water was excruciatingly clear, the air was dead calm and the sun was bright. There wasn't a cloud in the sky except for a few wispy mare's tails clinging to the peaks of the Williams Fork Mountains on the eastern horizon, where they'd do us no good at all.

Mark said most of the water would be too low to fish this late in the season and that our best shot for trout would be in the big beaver pond at the head of the creek. On the way up there, he told me they didn't bring all their fishermen here because even in less demanding conditions it takes at least decent casting and a minimum of finesse to fish it. I think he meant that as fair warning.

29

I don't estimate the size of ponds well, but I'll say this one covered more than one acre, but less then two. (Or maybe more than two acres, but less than three.) There's no telling how deep it was, but by late summer the weed tops had grown to within inches of the surface. There was a small pod of apparently large trout boiling out at the end of what looked like my longest cast and a few others working above the beaver dam off to our left. Wading closer was out of the question. In water like this you'd sink to your armpits in black muck within three steps, and even if you didn't, your spreading ripples would spook the fish.

Buzz teetered out on the beaver dam, while Mark and I cast side by side, trying a dozen fly patterns between us with no luck: midge pupae, mayfly nymphs, beetles, ants, backswimmers, damselflies. Buzz hooked a big trout on a little grasshopper pattern, but it took him into the weeds and broke him off. I finally hooked a heavy fish on a size 20 soft hackle. It made a good run, peeling off line, then did an about-face and swam straight back at me. It was the kind of maneuver that makes you suspect that the fish not only comprehends the nature of his problem, but is also considerably smarter than you are. By the time I recovered my slack line, the barbless hook had come loose and the commotion had spooked the pond.

Buzz went back to work, and Mark and I drove to the freestone creek, where we lounged in the pickup eating leftover fried chicken and listening to grasshoppers clicking in the hay meadow. The stream was a pretty little thing meandering widely across the meadow, taking its own sweet time before it emptied into the river. There was a deep undercut bank at the outside of every bend and we caught fat brown trout and one cuttbow in most of the spots where you'd expect them to be. There were no refusal rises. The trout ate our hoppers as if they'd been waiting for them all morning, which in fact they probably had. This didn't look like what you'd call a rich stream, and fish of that size probably weren't residents but trout that had moved up out of the river to gorge on grasshoppers in the late summer. They wouldn't have been here in the spring, and they'd probably be gone back to the river by the middle of next month when the hopper supply ran out.

I've always wondered how fish know to do things like that. Do they understand their environment to the extent that they can formulate a plan? We fishermen constantly overestimate the intelligence of fish so that matching wits with them doesn't seem too ridiculous, but at the risk of selling the fish short, that seems doubtful. I think trout are more like your average fisherman: They snoop around because it's in their nature and they're just smart enough to know when they've stumbled into something good.

4

COASTERS

I came to know about Michigan's Upper Peninsula through the writing of Ernest Hemingway, John Voelker (a.k.a. Robert Traver) and later Jim Harrison and others. It may be a coincidence that many of the writers I like have a connection to this northernmost landmass of Michigan that, until the completion of the Mackinac Bridge in 1957, was so isolated it could be reached from the rest of the state only by boat. Or maybe it's that the region naturally produces stories filled with tea-colored trout streams, beaver ponds hidden in swamps and small towns where rules are gracefully bent by those with the right intentions. Whatever the reason, the UP is enshrined alongside the Serengeti, the Yukon Territory and Paris as a place made romantic by virtue of appearing in books. Which is to say, I am an innocent victim of literature.

I'm less sure where I first heard about coasters, the adfluvial brook trout that spawn in streams and then use Lake Superior to feed and grow the way anadromous fish like salmon use an ocean. They're an item of local knowledge, not something you'd expect to hear about out here in Colorado. If you're a fisherman living in any of the three U.S. states and one Canadian province bordering Lake Superior, there's a good chance you know what a coaster is. Otherwise, you'll probably think it's the thing your mother makes you put under your glass of iced tea.

These fish were said to be elusive, coming and going mysteriously in the largest, deepest and coldest of the Great Lakes, and they could get big. The world-record brook trout—the fourteen-pound, eight-ounce slab caught in 1917—was a coaster that had fattened up in Lake Superior before returning to the Nipigon River in Ontario. Of course a world record is an impossible standard—especially one that was caught almost a century ago—but word is that even in these benighted times a twenty-inch-plus fish might not be out of the question. And then there *is* that photo of a more recently caught coaster brookie that's going around the Internet. It's a big, sloppy hog of a fish that wasn't weighed before it was released but that the length-and-girth formula suggests would have come in at a stupefying sixteen pounds. Or so the story goes.

So when Bill Bellinger called to ask if I wanted to meet him in the UP in early June to fish, I asked the same question I'd asked several other friends in the area: "Do you know anything about coasters?" Instead of the usual, "I've heard of 'em, but have never caught 'em,"

Bill said, "Oh, sure. I got into 'em the same time last year on size 12 flying ants."

I booked a flight to Marquette. I tied no less than a dozen size 12 flying ants. You know how it is.

I'd met Bill fifteen years ago when I was in Charlevoix, Michigan, for a funeral. In the course of things, I ended up with a few free days, and it was suggested I go fishing, possibly to get me out from underfoot so cooler heads could deal with the adult business. When I asked around about a guide, everyone steered me toward Bill, or "Wild Bill," as he was known then.

He turned out to be a competent young guy with a little house on the river, a bulldog named Killian (after a brand of beer) and a beautiful wooden Au Sable River boat. We floated the Jordan River and I caught some fish. The next day I borrowed a car and followed Bill's detailed directions to some beaver ponds, where I caught more fish and didn't see another person all day. I won't go so far as to say that everything was suddenly okay. Death isn't just a big deal; it's *the* big deal. Still, life does go on.

I didn't see Bill again until I got off the plane in Marquette. I wasn't sure I'd recognize him, but there he was, looking not much older and standing next to a teenager he introduced as Sam Black—known as "Sammy"—who'd be fishing with us. Sammy was a compact, broad-shouldered, sixteen-year-old hockey player and avid fisherman: the son of a neighbor whose father was "out of the picture" for the usual complicated reasons. In the kind of rural volunteerism that still exists in northern Michigan, Bill had stepped in to take up some of the slack.

It was better than an hour's drive to the borrowed cabin where we'd be staying, so there was time to catch up. (Aside from having fished together, Bill and I are connected by a web of common acquaintances that fall just short of shirttail relations.) It turned out that everyone was doing either okay or as well as could be expected under the circumstances.

Bill himself was no longer Wild Bill the single fishing guide, but a married housepainter. That didn't seem to have changed him much, although there *is* a prenuptial agreement stating that Bill can come and go as he pleases as long as he's fishing or hunting, but he can't walk into a bar without his wife on his arm.

We'd planned to go out in the sixteen-foot boat Bill had trailered up, but it was windy and rainy and Superior was too rough. So we parked the boat at the cabin and threaded our way down a muddy two-track to a point about 150 feet above the lake. The shoreline for miles along here is mostly sheer sandstone cliffs right down to the water, but in this one spot you can pick your way down to the water and cast from a convenient boulder pile.

I felt good about the whole deal. This was where Bill had caught fish a year ago, and the guy at the sporting goods store in the small town of Big Bay had allowed as how it was as good a place as any for coasters. Beyond that we'd hit the usual cagey stonewall where the local fisherman sniffs out what the out-of-towners already know and then leads them to believe that that's pretty much the whole story.

I was glad we hadn't tried to go out in the boat. The waves were high enough along this shore that the crests would break at our feet, splashing our boots, and the troughs would reveal ten feet of bare rock below us. I left the flying ants in the box—figuring no fish would rise in such heavy seas—and tied on a large streamer. I quickly figured out that I could add a dozen feet to my longest throw by casting as a wave broke and then feeding line as it receded.

In the end, Bill and I cast until our arms hurt without so much as a bump, while Sammy, fishing a worm and bobber on a spinning rod, landed and released a whitefish and a small coaster. I congratulated him and Bill proudly clapped him on the shoulder. Sammy didn't seem to know what to do with all this praise.

The weather that week was the way it can be on the south shore of Lake Superior. There were none of the epic storms known locally as "Canadian crap hammers," but there was a steady parade of rainy, windy squalls that would either keep us off the big lake altogether or make us leery about going around the western point of the bay toward the mouth of the Salmon Trout River. As we got close to the point some days, we could see the shear line where the waves got much bigger than the ones we were already bobbing in, which were plenty big enough, thank you. We were in a sixteen-foot open boat and the water temperature was around forty degrees. Sometimes I think I've grown overly cautious as I've gotten older. Other times I think that's *how* I've gotten older.

None of us knew a lot about coasters, but we did know a few things through common wisdom. One was that the Salmon Trout was the last remaining coaster river in the UP. Another was that once the fish move out into Lake Superior, they stick tight to the coast—hence the name—in relatively shallow water over a rubble rock bottom where your odds of catching them aren't all that good. Casey Huckins, a biology professor at Michigan Tech who has studied this population, told me that there are no more than 150 Salmon Trout coasters in the lake at any one time and that they can spread out over roughly fifty miles of shoreline. That would work out to about three fish per mile if they were distributed evenly, which of course they're not.

We developed the ritual of standing in front of our cabin in the mornings drinking coffee and studying the cliffs across the bay that we wanted to fish. They were two miles away, but when the wind was up, we could see the uneven white line of waves breaking against them and knew we'd be off to the Yellow Dog River until the weather cleared, or maybe to a pretty beaver pond Bill swore wasn't private, even though getting on it involved climbing through a convenient hole in a chain-link fence.

We got out on the big lake in fits and starts—a morning here, an afternoon there, as storms and waves allowed. Bill and Sammy had the procedure at the boat launch down to a science, so I was left with the simple job of stuffing the two-dollar launch fee in the envelope provided and filling in the blanks. Date: June something. Make of vehicle: Chevy. Name: Bellinger. And Bill's license number, which was easy to remember: 4ZTROUT.

The fishing was what you'd call methodical. We'd slow-troll along the cliffs, casting streamers toward shore and stripping them back. Takes were few and far between, so I concentrated on my casting: the unhurried drift on the back cast, the smooth punch and haul on the forward stroke, with a glance at the deck to see if I was standing on my loose line. It became obvious that this was another one of those fish-of-a-thousand-casts deals, so the job was to make clean throws one after another and not to be asleep at the wheel from monotony when the strike finally came.

We did our best when we could tuck our flies right up against the cliffs in shallow water, but that wasn't always possible. Some days the rollers were high enough that you could lose depth in a trough and tick the uneven bottom with the skeg if you got in too close. These same waves could also put you on the rocks in minutes if the outboard stalled, and Bill's outboard, though serviceable, wasn't above overheating and stalling from time to time. So we stayed in deeper water and lobbed streamers as far as we could reach into the shallows. Bill explained all this to Sammy, who eagerly soaked it up. Whatever was or wasn't going on at home, this was a kid who wouldn't have to try to piece together the fine points of fishing from magazines and instructional DVDs.

The fish we hooked and got to the boat were recognizable early summer coasters: strong and chunky, mostly sixteen or seventeen inches long and a pale grayish-silver in color. The typical brook trout markings were all there, and later in the year as spawning approached, they'd color up like small stream brookies, but now they looked washed-out, overexposed.

Professor Huckins said these early-season fish look too much like splake for their own good and are sometimes mistakenly kept by fishermen who aren't paying close attention. ("Know your fish," the state fishing regulations implore.) The limit on coasters is one fish no less than twenty inches long. In the waters we were fishing, splake can be kept at fifteen inches and you can string up three. Huckins isn't a fan of splake. He said that even without the chronic case of mistaken identity, it doesn't make sense to pollute the gene pool by stocking a fertile hybrid of lake trout and brook trout in a fishery that already has spawning populations of both fish.

The coasters' original range isn't precisely known, but the best guess is that most of the three hundred–plus rivers and streams feeding Lake Superior once had healthy spawning populations. Using the fifty-mile range of the Salmon Trout fish as a rule of thumb, it's easy to picture them in the early 1800s spread out along the lake's entire 2,726 miles of coast, plus inshore shoals and islands.

By the turn of the last century, much of the coaster habitat had been or was about to be degraded or destroyed outright by road and railway construction, mining, logging and hydroelectric dams, but even before that they were hit hard by fishermen. Commercial fishing began early and the haul can only be guessed at. Records either weren't kept or haven't survived, and even when they do exist, lakers and coasters were often lumped together under the single heading of "trout."

The extent of the hook-and-line catch is also unknown, but the evidence is everywhere in old mounts of large brook trout and sepia-tone photos of grinning dudes from Detroit or Chicago posing with obscene piles of big, dead fish. It's hard not to envy those guys, not so much for the fishing they had, but for their innocence. When you bring a coaster to the boat today, you know you're looking at a member of a remnant population and you can't help feeling something short of guilt, but a little past nostalgia.

And the threats to the coasters' habitat aren't all in the past. The Kennecott Minerals Company is currently digging a copper mine in the headwaters of the Salmon Trout River—the last coaster river in Michigan, remember—which, according to the opposition, could destroy the fishery through siltation and the introduction of sulfuric acid, both unavoidable byproducts of sulfide mining. According to the company, the proper environmental safeguards are in place and everything will be fine. The environmentalists counter that, to date, there has never been a sulfide copper mine near a river where pollution didn't occur. And so on.

We got an earful about this from Gene and Carla, our neighbors in the next cabin down the shore. They'd moved to the UP when they retired, but their plans for a quiet life of fishing, kayaking and snowshoeing had been sidetracked by unexpected new careers as unpaid environmental activists. It was a familiar story: a small group of underfunded locals who were long on outrage and short on strategy up against a multinational corporation with the kind of lawyers who, as someone once said, could get a sodomy charge reduced to tailgating. As you might expect, things hadn't gone well. The opposition was not only outgunned and underfunded, but Michigan has a long history of being sympathetic to extractive industries and careless of the environment. If nothing else, you know what you're up against when the local newspaper is called the *Mining Journal*.

One afternoon when we'd been blown off the lake again, Gene drove us to look at the mine site. He'd given the impression that there was still a chance to stop the project, but it looked like a done deal to me. There were high chain-link fences plastered with KEEP OUT signs, heavy equipment everywhere and diesel exhaust in the air. The narrow dirt road we'd driven in on was in the process of being widened to superhighway proportions. Several guys in hard hats recognized Gene and gave him the hairy eyeball reserved for tree huggers bent on stopping progress.

We drove slowly past the mine to where the Salmon Trout went under the road through a culvert. At this point the river was narrow enough to jump across, flowing out of an expanse of jack pine and alder. Bill walked into the woods and came back in a few minutes to report that there were small brook trout fining in a couple of pools. He wondered if there might be beaver ponds up here somewhere that held bigger fish. Gene was silently glum, leaning against the car with his hands in his pockets. I was uncomfortably contemplating my personal use of copper (I must have gone through pounds of the stuff for the ribs on nymphs alone). Sammy took it all in with an air of puzzlement. I got the sense that he'd rather just fish without all these complications. Me too, kid.

As soon as we got back in cellphone range on the drive home, Gene called Carla. She answered with, "Did you get arrested again?" and he replied, "Not this time." This may or may not have been a private joke.

One calm afternoon we motored out of the bay, past the mouth of the river, and found a small pod of coasters off a spectacular rocky point. I'd just caught a nice one from under a rock overhang when a man in a canoe paddled over. His name was Paul; he was a self-confessed coaster fanatic and a member of the Huron Mountain Club, which owns the entire fishable length of the Salmon Trout. After a few minutes of conversation, he asked if we'd like to fish the river. We said okay.

Lower down it was deep, slow, brush-choked and estuarine, but higher up it was a pretty little trout river flowing through some of the last old-growth forest in the UP. Below a waterfall that formed a natural barrier, we caught some eight-to-ten-inch brookies that you'd have to describe as coaster smolts.

Later, Paul showed us an old skin mount of a coaster from the late 1800s. A large brook trout—maybe six or seven pounds—had been skinned in one piece with the skill of a Beverly Hills plastic surgeon, and the skin had been sewn onto a piece of birch bark with something that looked like sinew but might have been waxed twine. The white birch bark showed spookily through the empty eye socket. There was no approximation of life here as in modern taxidermy. This thing had been dead for over a century and looked it.

I'd heard about the Huron Mountain Club only a week ago, so I had to be told how unbelievable it was to be given access. The club was started by wealthy industrialists (some might say robber barons), it covers almost the entire Huron Mountain range and it's always been jealous if not downright paranoid about its privacy. Lots of sporting clubs bill themselves as venerable and exclusive, but few can boast of a founding date of 1889 or of making Henry Ford himself wait six years to be accepted as a member.

The club is an almost mythical presence to locals. Some who have lived nearby all their lives claim to know nothing about it. Others tell of hidden motion sensors and armed thugs who descend on trespassers like the wrath of God. Maybe, maybe not, but there *is* a padlocked gate and a guard shack manned twenty-four hours a day by guys who never smile.

Still others claim to have brazenly waltzed on more than once to fish the river without getting caught. Again—maybe, maybe not. Stories about poaching remind me of the tales of sexual conquest I heard in high school. No doubt those adventures did happen, but maybe not at quite the frequency or the fever pitch you're led to believe.

On the way back to the cabin that evening, Bill said to Sammy, "Someday you'll tell your grandchildren you fished the Huron Mountain Club *with permission.*"

The next day, back on the lake, Bill had a close call with a big coaster. The fish boiled up after a streamer, darting and nipping as if it knew there was a hook and wanted to bite the thing in a safe place.

The fish was on briefly—long enough to put a deep bow in the rod—
and then he threw the hook close to the boat. He was big. Twenty
inches easy, maybe twenty-one or twenty-two. This would have been
a rare keeper, but although we never talked about it, I don't think Bill
would have kept the fish.

Somewhere on the drive down to the airport in Marquette, where
they dropped me off, Sammy asked what we thought would happen
with the coasters. We said we didn't know, that it didn't look good,
but could still go either way, which struck us all as an honest but
unsatisfying answer. Then Bill tried to lighten things up by saying,
"Maybe someday you'll tell your grandchildren you caught coasters
when they were still in the UP."

I glanced at Sammy in the back seat in time to catch his look.
Grandchildren again. I remember age sixteen. You knew there was a
long haul in front of you, but spans of time large enough to encom-
pass marriage, children and grandchildren, let alone the possible
extinction of an entire fish population, seemed too theoretical to
contemplate. And anyway, there were things closer at hand to think
about, like the next hockey game, the next fishing trip and that blond
girl in study hall—not necessarily in that order.

5

THIS YEAR'S FLY

The best motel in Basalt, Colorado, is the Green Drake. It's clean, plain, not too expensive and you can guess from the name that fishermen are welcome. The resident dog is named Baxter. He's a hundred-pound yellow Lab and a friendly and sudden leaner. You quickly learn that when you stop to pet him you have to throw a leg out and brace yourself so he doesn't knock you over.

You'd have to describe the place as homey, but it hasn't entirely escaped the gentrification that's occurred in the twenty-five years

45

since Basalt was the workingman's alternative to nearby Aspen. In almost any other town in the West, this establishment would be called the Green Drake Motel, but here it's The Green Drake: A Motel.

April can be one of the heaviest snow months in the Colorado Rockies, so at this time of year the drive over from the East Slope is a crap shoot that takes between four and eight hours depending on the weather in the passes. With luck, we—my buddies Doug and Vince and I—pull into town by midmorning, check into the Drake and stop at the fly shop to say hello, pick up the latest fishing report and buy half a dozen of this year's fly.

Last year's fly was the Hatching Midge: a plastic-winged, trailing-husk pattern that I thought had too many body parts for the size 18 and 20 hooks it was tied on. I said it was the kind of self-consciously pretty fly designed to catch more fishermen than fish, bought some anyway and caught almost all my trout on them. This year's fly is the Morgan's Midge. I buy the usual half dozen without comment.

The next stop is the convenience store for a thermos of coffee and a gut bomb to go for lunch. When it's all said and done, we make the river on that first day for the second half of the banker's hours hatch. By the time we get up there, many of the well-known pools are taken, but it's a workday, the weekend crowd has thinned out and there's plenty of water to choose from. It helps that the three of us have seventy years of combined experience on this river. Chances are good that we'll find a few overlooked pods of risers and catch a few trout, and in fact we do.

The guy at the fly shop had said, "There's no reason to be on the river before ten-thirty," so the next morning we're fed, rigged up and on the water by half past nine. This is such an old and obvious trick that it shouldn't work anymore, but it still does, as often as not. We spread out in two of the best pools on the river and kill an hour sipping coffee as cars filled with guides and fishermen slow down, spot us and then speed up again, heading to their second choice.

Doug and Vince have gone upstream to grab a spot that will keep two fishermen busy through an entire hatch. There's a long pool with a wide tailout below an even longer riffly run. This whole stretch is lousy with trout, it pumps out flies like a factory and it's a rare day when there's no one fishing it. I can't see Doug and Vince from where I am, but I know that one of them has taken the pool and the other has staked out the riffle: positioning themselves to block anyone working in from above or below.

This is a famous and often heavily fished river: one of Colorado's best and some say *the* best for dry flies. It's not exactly combat fishing, but you do pick up certain passive-aggressive techniques. Grabbing your spot early is one. Parking smack in the middle of small turnouts so there's no room for another car to squeeze in on either side is another, not to mention fishing in the shoulder seasons when there aren't as many tourists around. That kind of thing.

I've volunteered to fish a smaller spot downstream. This isn't much of a run, but the sweet spot is a small back eddy against the far bank. If you could wade four feet closer to it, you could get a decent high-stick, dapping dry-fly drift, but you're stopped short by a steep drop-off, so you're reduced to trying for a severe pile cast with a hard left-handed aerial mend.

I've been fascinated by this spot since I first fished it in the mid-1970s. The first time I saw it, I said to the guy I was with, "I can't make that cast." He replied, "Me neither, but if we don't try, we'll never learn." Thirty-some years later there are days when I still can't make the cast and others when I can just manage it. I've caught a few nice big trout there, plus others that were smaller, but still on the high side of average. Two fish is the best I've ever done, although even one fish constitutes a victory and on days when the wind buggers my cast or I'm just off my game, I've spooked the pool with dragging flies and gone away skunked. It's a good place to start the day because everything else will be easier.

That morning I go through the normal drill. I tie on the Morgan's

Midge that worked yesterday, wait for the hatch to start and then wait a while longer, until three trout start rising in the eddy and get into a rhythm. Then I wade out to the shelf, manage several passable drifts and get a thick, heavy fifteen-inch rainbow. He puts up a good tussle on 7x tippet, and at one point I think he'll get into the next riffle and run me downstream, but then he stops in the tailout and I land him where I stand.

The commotion puts down the other two fish, so I wade to shore and sit on a flat rock that's been polished by eons of flowing water with a final buffing applied by the asses of fishermen clad first in canvas, then latex, then neoprene and lately Gore-Tex. I check my leader for nicks and wind knots, cut off my fly and tie it back on with a fresh knot, think about cleaning my line but don't, and try the coffee I've left in an insulated cup on the bank, but it's stone cold. Those other two trout back in the eddy still haven't started rising again and I don't feel like wasting the hatch waiting for them, so I walk up to horn in on Doug and Vince. The stretch they're fishing is big enough for two strangers or three close friends.

Not counting that first day when we're in a hurry to get to the river, we brew our own coffee, pack our own lunches and do as much cooking as possible in the room to save money. But we always eat breakfast at the Two Rivers Café. It's half a block from the motel and it's the last café in town that opens early and that hasn't morphed into a "bistro" and tripled its prices. There are two schools of thought when it comes to breakfast. I've seen Vince start a day of fishing on a bowl of oatmeal, which is fine if you like that sort of thing. But then the hatch can last until three on a good day, which makes it a long way till lunch, so I tend toward eggs, grits, sausage and biscuits at a minimum, adding flapjacks if the weather is cold.

This year it's sunny, chilly in the mornings and in the high forties by early afternoon. The same week last year we white-knuckled over the mountains in a moderate blizzard and fished for four days in steadily falling snow and knee-deep drifts. I'll take either extreme or anything in between as long as the midges are hatching, but all fishing weather can have its advantages.

Midges have been known to hatch heavily on gray, cold days, and trout can be more aggressive when the light is low. Wind sucks for casting (it's always coming from the wrong direction), but it can mash the flies onto the surface and get the fish gorging on cripples. Trout can be skittish on bright, sunny days, but you have the benefit of being able to spot them in the clear water.

After a childhood spent lowering worms out of sight into dark water, I've become a sucker for the visual stuff, which is the only real reason I prefer dry flies to nymphs. I'll never get over the sight of a trout coming off the bottom in three feet of clear water to eat, or at least look at my fly. Once you get accustomed to this quick glimpse, you can tell if it's a brown or a rainbow and get a good sense of its size, all in the space of a split second. The brilliant high-altitude sunlight that allows that to happen is also what gives Colorado its high incidence of skin cancer, which is why the wide-brimmed fishing hat is not entirely an affectation. You may look like a doofus, but you're more likely to keep your ears and nose well into your seventies.

The Morgan's Midge produced well, as advertised, but one day at a long run known as Rosie's, I locate a pod of rising trout that don't like it. Of course, this isn't unheard of. This is the kind of small, technical river where not even the right fly works all the time and where you'll now and then see fish refuse naturals out of general paranoia. Still, a fly that's been working usually fools two or three trout out of a pod of a dozen or fifteen steady risers.

Just for the hell of it, I try the Hatching Midge. I get a brief glance and what looks like a shrug from one small brown, but that's it. No surprise there. These are fashion-conscious trout that would no sooner eat last year's fly than they'd wear white after Labor Day.

The Morgan's Midge I've been using consists of a short trailing husk made of two or three strands of fine, root-beer-colored tinsel, a gray thread body, a stubby wing made of gray CDC and a sparse grizzly parachute hackle tied around a white foam wing post. The post is then cut off flush, leaving a tiny white button that, amazingly, can often be spotted on the water at a range of forty feet or more. I tie the ratty one I'd been using back on my tippet, and in a fit of creativity, cut the wing off with my nippers. Of course you've crossed some kind of line when you start trimming pieces off a size 22 fly because it's too bushy, but that's what we've come to on some tailwaters where sophisticated tackle and heavy fishing pressure have made the fish preternaturally selective.

I catch four trout in seven casts with the wingless fly and then it starts fluttering weirdly on the false cast. When I strip it in, I find that the hackle has come loose and is sticking out to the side. This had been a well-tied fly that had stayed together through something like twenty trout, but nothing lasts forever. I reach for my nippers to cut off the fly and put on a fresh one, then get a wild hair, nip off the hackle and fish it that way. There isn't much left of the fly now—just the trailing husk, some thread and that little foam button—but it works better than it had before. I get four or five more trout on it before I finally spook the pod.

On the way back to town that afternoon, we stop to see my friend Roy Palm. Roy lives on a private stretch of river—a quarter mile or so of some of the prettiest and fishiest water in the valley—but he's not one of the wealthy landowners who've arrived in recent decades. In fact, he's an old river rat who wangled his way onto this property in the late sixties or early seventies and has held on through a series of maneuvers that would have given a Wall Street banker a migraine.

Since then he's largely left the streambed alone, but he's taken some small browns out to avoid overcrowding and keep the size up and he did build a head-gate-controlled side channel so wild fish from downstream can spawn unmolested. He also built benches at several of the best runs for solitary river watching. When I first fished this property, it was a jungle of willow and cottonwood saplings, but in recent years the banks have gotten more manicured. It's easier to fish now, but less wild-looking. There's been a revolving roster of hunting dogs around the place and two of them—both yellow Labs—are buried in neatly marked graves above the high water line at a place called the Tree Pool. I remember them both as pups, especially Flicka, who once ate my hat.

Over the years Roy has done every job imaginable to get by, but since I've known him he's guided, owned and run fly shops and tied flies professionally. Many of the standard flies on the river first came from his vise (including some rustled patterns that now bear other people's names). His flies were always admirably spare and simple, but now that he's more or less retired and no longer worries about selling flies, his patterns have become totally minimalist. The last batch he showed me consisted of nearly naked hooks with a little thread and a wisp of wing or a half turn of hackle: just the barest suggestion of an insect. These flies aren't what you'd call commercially viable, but they're deadly, and their delicacy would be startling even if they hadn't come from the big hands of a man who looks, sounds and sometimes acts like a bear.

Roy's fishing seems to have gone in that same direction. He was never a fish hog, but by now a day of fishing consists mostly of watching fish feed, examining insects on the water and then tinkering at the vise. He might catch a trout or two to test a pattern, but then he'll retire to one of the benches again to watch and think—usually with his two current Labs and a fresh drink. Roy reminds me of a character in a James Crumley novel who had "a heart as big as all outdoors—and a liver as big as a salmon."

You could say that Roy is proprietary about this stretch of river. He's been fairly generous with access over the years—more generous than I would have been—but when someone has an especially good day, he might mosey out to announce that they've caught enough of his babies and it's time to quit. They probably felt pleasantly alone up till then, but at that moment they realized they'd been under surveillance the whole time.

It's widely believed that Roy shoots at trespassers, but that's not strictly true, although he does have rifle targets set up at strategic places along the river, so that if you *were* trespassing, you might inadvertently stumble into the line of fire of his flat-shooting varmint rifle. Technically speaking, that would be an unfortunate coincidence. When the sheriff stopped by after one incident, Roy shrugged and said, "There ain't supposed to be anyone back there."

We sit on the back porch drinking coffee and talking for an hour or so, and then Roy invites us to come back and fish there the next day.

We show up at ten-thirty the following morning and spend what seems like half the hatch walking the river as Roy points out, in excruciating detail, how insect drift lines, currents and holding water came together into specific feeding lanes, with special emphasis on the quiet, bank-hugging seams you could easily miss.

This is knowledge accumulated over decades spent watching more and fishing less, and although I've fished this place myself off and on for thirty years, I'm learning things I hadn't yet figured out. So I listen attentively, but it takes the better part of an hour, fish are feeding the whole time and I begin to get a little twitchy. I'm not a fish hog either, and I do aspire to the enlightened vantage point that would let me watch trout rise without wanting to cast to them. Still, my internal voice keeps saying, "Dude, get a hook in the water!"

When the tour is finally over, I wade into the shelving riffle above the Camp Pool and tie on a Morgan's Midge. I've clipped the wings off all the ones I have left, but I've provisionally left the hackles on because, although I now know better, I still like all the little bells and whistles. I pick my fish and land eight or nine real nice ones before the hatch peters out. I don't know if Roy is watching or not, but I suspect this is a number he'd consider appropriate.

6

NEW WATER

Like most of the trout streams in my life, I first saw this one from the window of a moving car. We were at right angles to each other at a narrow bridge, going our separate ways. It was just a sidelong glance: not much more than a fisherman at the wheel registering flowing water off his left shoulder.

Farther along, the road turned to roughly parallel the stream and there were longer glimpses through the trees and then full views. In this stretch it was mostly riffles with uniform cobble bottoms and darker slots at the bends where fish would hold. I followed it downstream as it took on small tributaries with unremarkable names like Willow, Spruce, Moose, Buck, Bear, and Boulder creeks and grew from a creek itself to a good-sized stream and finally to a proper little river.

This was a stream I'd heard of in passing. It was said to be no more than ordinary cutthroat trout water, and with bigger, more fashionable rivers in the neighborhood, it wasn't crowded. I remember seeing a few fly fishers, but they didn't look like the fancy kind. Most wore ditch boots and no vests. One guy was wading wet in blue jeans. With a Stetson pulled down to shade his eyes, he looked like a sleepy cowpoke in a Charles Russell painting. But although this was a good time of year to fish and the stream was clear and at a nice flow, there were miles of open water and dozens of pull-offs where no cars were parked.

At a crossroads at the bottom of the canyon, I stopped to get gas and coffee and, being endlessly curious about the headwaters of trout streams, I traced the stream backward on a map. It flowed in from the west, where it crossed contour lines and gathered the shorter blue lines of a few smaller creeks. It ran under the road at the bridge, where I first saw it and then made a dogleg to the north against a ridge. Upstream of the bridge, the stream drained part of one mountain range; downstream it drained part of another. Altogether it was an area of something like thirteen hundred square miles. So many roads in the West are built along streams and rivers that you can begin to picture the place as wetter than it really is, but you get a clearer sense of the preciousness of water when you stop to think how little of it has run off that much land.

As with all mountain streams, this one seemed isolated high up in its own watershed. It took a conscious act of will to imagine it going on to join a larger river, which joined a larger one yet and so on for well over a thousand river miles to the coast. Before dams and head gates, you could have floated a pinecone all the way from here to the Pacific. Once upon a time, steelhead migrated from the coast to within less than a hundred miles of where I stood stretching my legs and studying a map before hurrying on my way.

This road isn't a main route to anywhere in particular unless you're a fisherman, but I *am* a fisherman, so I saw the stream other times over the next dozen years or so, always from a car window and always on my way elsewhere. It became part of my personal map of the region, which is simple-mindedly all about watercourses. It always looked interesting, but somehow never quite interesting enough to make me change my plans. I guess I'd hit one of those patches where my fishing had become purposeful and I'd temporarily lost the playful aimlessness of someone with all the time in the world.

I finally fished it higher up on the drainage with a friend. It just happened, in the way of things that are long overdue. We were in the neighborhood anyway and for once we were in no hurry. My friend knew a landowner, called in a favor and we ended up on a stretch of water above that first bridge that I'd never seen before but that I might have picked off the map as a likely sweet spot.

Upstream of where we fished, it was a mountain creek that tumbled down through twenty miles and several thousand feet of mixed spruce and pine woods on Forest Service land. There were a few places where you could four-wheel down to it, each with well-worn old campsites, but most of it was temptingly roadless: miles and miles of small, trouty-looking pocket water.

Downstream of that, it flowed out across fifteen miles of pastureland in a small, open valley. Here it slowed and stretched out into pools, riffles and wide meanders extensive enough to cover nearly twice the length of its own valley with the prettiest little western trout stream you'll ever see. The mountain range upstream to the west loomed. Its signature 10,000-foot peak was ten miles away, but in the clear, thin air it looked close enough to hit it with a rock. The mountains downstream were higher and craggier, but even at a range of thirty miles you could still pick out distinct snowfields. I moved to the Rocky Mountains forty-two years ago and have been here as a more or less successful transplant ever since. I suppose I now take it all for granted almost as much as those who were born here, but every once in a while I see something like this and remember why I don't live in Cleveland.

This was a more or less intact working ranch that covered most of the small valley. It was exactly the kind of place you'd have settled yourself, but not for the beautiful trout stream as you now think. Back in the old days you'd have been a hard-bitten homesteader with an eye to cattle, so you'd have seen water for stock and to flood-irrigate hay, plus handy lumber that could be skidded off the hillsides and free food in the form of deer and elk. You'd have ended up with the entire valley not because you had delusions of grandeur—although that may also have been true—but because you'd need every last square foot of that poor pasturage to make a spread pay. The trout in the stream would have meant nothing more than the odd afternoon off and a break from a steady diet of red meat.

I'll never get over the feeling of approaching a stream for the first time. I like it best when I can walk up on it from a distance, say five hundred yards through sage and prairie grass scattered with summer wildflowers. I can't see or hear water yet, but up ahead the brush thickens into willows and a broken tree line of juniper, pine and cottonwood where the stream has to be. I'll saunter along acting nonchalant, but the anticipation is palpable.

Maybe I'll flush grasshoppers ahead of me and think hard about that, but I try never to tie on a fly before I have a close look at the water. Chances are I know what I'm doing and what will work, but tying on a fly too soon indicates the kind of false confidence that could cost me later. I remind myself that every day of fishing plays out like a movie. I may be hoping for something like *My Dinner with Andre*, but it could always turn out to be *Dude, Where's My Car?*

My friend and I came on the stream at a shallow riffle with a bend pool upstream and the glassy tail of a bigger pool just visible above that. At first it seemed bigger than I expected it to be this high up on the drainage. Then, after only a few seconds, it seemed to be exactly the right size. We split up there and I forced myself to ritually watch the water for five whole minutes on general principles. The best fishermen I know are all cool customers who take their own sweet time, and even on days like this when I don't feel the requisite stillness, I try my best to fake it.

This was a high-altitude-meadow stream at a perfect clear, late summer flow, running mostly in the open between the exposed gravel of its own high water line, but shouldering up against dark, root-bound cut banks on the outsides of bends. It was morning on a day that would reach into the low eighties with a deep blue sky and cumulonimbus clouds the shape and color of cotton balls. This was an entirely recognizable medium-sized trout stream, but it would have a few peculiarities of its own that I didn't want to overlook by being in a hurry. I also wanted to take a moment to wonder how I'd managed to drive right past this lovely little thing so many times over so many years on my way to something I thought would be better.

There were a few odd mayflies and caddis in the air, but nothing you could call a hatch and no trout rising. So it came down to what I was in the mood for. On an out-of-the-way freestone stream like this, any number of things can work, but did I want to bank on the mysterious, unseen pluck to a nymph, the bulge to an emerger, the considered sip to a dry fly or the splashy lunge to a hopper? With nothing much to go on, I picked two old standards: a medium-sized, drably colored parachute dry fly and an equally nondescript nymph pattern on a dropper. The open secret to stream fishing is that your affection for your favorite fly patterns can be contagious.

I started casting methodically to cover the bend pool, first the slower current on the inside, then the faster main current, then a nice cast tight to the far bank in the deeper slack where I got a fish on. I'd been staring intently, but still somehow missed seeing if the fish took the dry or the dropper. All I knew was that something happened and I set on instinct.

This felt like a heavy trout, but it also didn't feel quite right. And then it was in the deep, fast current feeling weirdly logy as if it had me around a stick, and then it was coming up on the inside of the bend and I could see a good-sized fish being chased by a much bigger one. But then no, it was a big one on the dry fly and a slightly smaller fish on the nymph pulling in opposite directions. The big one was a nice big trout that I really wanted, but I had a light tippet and a 4-weight rod and two good fish on and this couldn't possibly end well. But then the smaller fish somehow got slack and threw the hook, and at that point the big one was just a rod's length away, so I slid it over to me and cradled it in my hand. It was a good seventeen inches long and it all happened just that fast, before either one of us had a chance to think it over.

I rolled the trout on its back to immobilize it, plucked out the barbless hook and then righted him in the current. He was sleek and firm: a muted greenish, grayish gold with the fine black pepper spots and orange chin slashes of a Snake River cutthroat. He rested just long enough to give me a good look before he squirted out of my loose grip. The fight couldn't have lasted more than a few seconds and the fish wasn't even tired, just a little confused.

So the conversation with this new water had begun and we'd hit it off nicely, like a first date that began with a clumsy exchange that we both thought was funny. I can't help but think of trout streams as feminine, but that's not some kind of left-handed gender politics. It's just that this kind of graceful and surprising sweetness calls to mind many of the women I know, but none of the men. Of course, strictly speaking, a trout stream is an inanimate object, but no fisherman really believes that.

I worked up the rest of that bend pool—another twenty yards or so—casting carefully and fully expecting another big cutthroat, but it didn't happen. Then I walked upstream to leapfrog my partner. He'd already fished the next long pool, worked up fifty yards of cut bank and was starting at the tail of the plunge pool above that. His normal fishing pace is faster than mine, but he's usually considerate enough not to rush too far ahead and has even been known to stop and wait if I fall too far behind. By way of holding up my end, I try to stifle my tendency to dawdle. We've fished together for years. It almost always works out.

I spent the next few hours in the state of mild surprise that always comes on a new stream—jumping between moments of rapt content-ment and the eagerness to see what comes next. There are many more similarities between trout streams than there are differences, but the differences are endlessly novel. A riffle is just a riffle, but the precise place where current speed, depth, bottom structure and drift lines conspire to make a good place for a trout to hold is always unique. The same goes for the cast that will send a fly down that slot without drag, while leaving the caster far enough away to keep from spooking the fish. Each new throw demands a moment of consider-ation. Hydrology is an open book, but it's a dense text that you don't always comprehend on the first reading.

As the morning warmed up, there were more insects around and the fish became more active. I began to spot the occasional trout sus-pended in the smooth tails of pools and saw the odd, unhurried rise. I switched out my dry and dropper rig, sticking with the same patterns, but in smaller, more realistic sizes. If a coherent hatch developed, I'd try my best to copy it out of my small stream box, but this didn't seem like that kind of water. This seemed like the kind that would grind out a sparse mixed bag of insects and where the trout would stay more or less open to a reasonable suggestion.

I've never quite come to terms with precision in fly fishing, which

I suppose is why I'm such an avid small-stream fisherman. A spring creek filled with clockwork hatches, quarter-inch-wide feeding lanes and highly selective trout is like a Swiss watch: a mechanism with such fine tolerances that you can't find a gap anywhere wide enough to slip in a single extra hackle fiber. A freestone stream seems like a clunkier device with gears that sometimes just barely mesh. A few turns of hackle or a hook size more or less usually won't matter, and if a trout decides he likes your fly, he'll swim a foot out of his way to eat it. This is the ideal place for the guy who thinks of himself simply as a fisherman rather than a "fish-catching machine," which in some circles is the ultimate compliment.

The fishing that day was never fast and furious, but it never slowed to what you could call a lull. The trout weren't exactly easy to catch, but for the most part they were right where you'd expect them to be and only a few presented the kind of puzzle that an adequate fly caster who's on his game couldn't solve. I never hooked another fish as big as that first one, but a few were in that same over-fifteen-inch class that can seem so big on small water.

There were no surprises, but somehow everything was a surprise: how the trout fit the water the way birds fit the air and how they're so hard to spot in the stream, but so ornately beautiful in the hand. I know their coloration is a practical matter of camouflage with a sea-sonal nod to mating, but there seems to be something else in opera-tion here: something frisky that has made these fish prettier than they'd have to be just to get by. It's fishing new water that lets me see all this again as if for the first time.

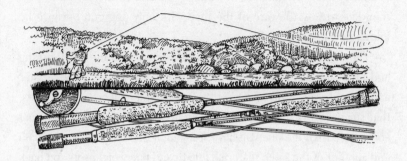

7

RODS

I got a rambling letter from a friend the other day talking about fly rods. *His* fly rods, that is, past and present: what they were, where they came from, where some of them eventually went (in recent years he's given some away to guides) and what he liked or didn't like about them. It was the kind of letter you write to a friend who shares your interest and who you don't have to impress—basically a two-page, stream-of-consciousness postscript.

There were surprisingly few rods considering that this man is a retired doctor in his late eighties and a lifelong fly fisher, but then not all of us are tackle freaks. I *am* a tackle freak, although after years of accumulating rods I've come to envy those who fish comfortably with what they have instead of always looking for something better. Marksmen like to say, "Beware of the man with only one gun because he knows how to use it."

The search for the perfect rod begins early in a life of fly fishing and often for the wrong reason. As a beginner, you're a poor caster and you naturally want to get better. In a commercial culture like ours, that suggests a better rod, which you are led to believe is a rod that costs more than the one you have. I mean, if one rod sells for $129.95 and another of the same material, length and line weight sets you back $700, why the difference in price if the expensive one isn't better? This is one of the burning philosophical questions of our time.

In fact, what you probably need are casting lessons, regular practice and, most of all, lots of fishing, since casting on water with fish in it is different from casting on a lawn, for reasons having to do with both physics and psychology. Also, there are things you'll learn on your own through constant exposure that no one could ever teach you.

But then in some rare cases, the rod you start with really *is* a clunker that holds you back. Maybe, as in my case, you bought it at a yard sale for a few dollars because that was all you could afford at the time. Before you handed over the money, you put the rod together and wiggled it as you'd seen others do, but that was just for show. You didn't know the first thing about fly rods, but you had the itch and had to start somewhere.

My first fly rod was a 7½-foot, four-piece fiberglass fly-spin combo with a reversible reel seat. Two rods for the price of one: What a deal! I wasn't much more than a kid at the time, but I still should have known that a tool that's supposed to do two separate jobs wouldn't do either of them very well. I did manage to catch some fish on this thing, but a kindly stranger who stopped one day to give me some much-needed casting tips ended the brief session by saying, "And when you get a few bucks running uphill, you really oughta get yourself a better rod." He was just trying to be helpful and he was right, but the idea that a new rod could improve my casting took root and ruined me for life. The obvious danger is that a fly rod—especially an expensive one—can be seen as a talisman with some inherent power of its own, while in practice it's more likely to be like a Stradivarius violin in the hands of someone who doesn't play well: a flawless instrument that nonetheless squawks like a chicken.

I did eventually get a rod that was better (almost anything would have been) and it proved to be the first of many. At that time I could have done virtually all my trout fishing with the 8-foot 5-weight Granger Victory I picked up for $50, but many of the fishing writers I was reading left the impression that doing all your fishing with one all-around rod was like performing brain surgery with a can opener. So I came to think I needed shorter 4- and 5-weights, longer 5- and 6-weights, 7-weight streamer rods, 8-weight bass rods, 9-weight salmon rods and so on, not to mention the reels and lines to go with them. Later, when I started traveling a lot, I backed up my two-piece rods with three-piece models that I could carry on airplanes. Then I gradually accumulated spares in case I broke one.

I developed the usual nit-picking preferences. I think a rod should be as long as possible for leverage and line mending and as short as it has to be for convenience. On my small home water, an 8½- or 9-foot rod is best for line control, but it's too long to cast in tight quarters or even to carry from pool to pool through thick woods. A 6½- or 7-foot rod is about the right length for casting but doesn't give you enough reach and leaves too much line on the water. Obviously the ideal rod for mountain creeks is 7 feet, 9 inches. That must be why I have four rods of that odd length: three 5-weights and a 4-weight.

My first good rods were all used split bamboo by defunct makers, but don't ask me why all these years later. It must have had something to do with my ideas about tradition, craftsmanship, romance and the dubious value of practicality in sport, not to mention the sense that we're too quick to leave the best we have behind us and call it progress. It was also a sign of the times when graphite was new, fiberglass was fading and bamboo was still a viable choice rather than a social statement.

Martin Keane hadn't yet published *Classic Rods and Rodmakers*, which started a price war on old bamboo that continued unevenly until the crash of 2008. It also helped that the Granger and Phillipson companies had been headquartered just down the road in Denver, and half the attics and garages in Colorado contained old bamboo rods that regularly turned up at yard sales with price tags in the $30-to-$50 range. That meant a working stiff could get his hands on them and still pay the rent, although sometimes just barely.

During that same period I just managed to afford a few longer Paynes (the shorter, lighter rods were already out of my reach), and as prices for the big-name makers went through the roof, I rightly guessed that F. E. Thomas rods would soon be sucked into the vacuum. I picked up two of them for a song: an 8-foot 4-weight and a 7½-foot 5-weight. Some of those rods would turn out to be the only good investments I ever made, and also hinted at the dark side of bamboo: Even those of us who claim not to care what they're worth can't help but be aware of their value and in weak moments can come off sounding like stockbrokers with hot tips.

At one point I even published a monograph on bamboo rods without realizing that this little book would mark me for life as a true believer. Some years later on a river in northern Canada, I met a man who said he was shocked to see me fishing a graphite rod. Shocked!

We're all children of our times. Bamboo spoke to me then and still does now, but if I took up fly fishing today, there's a good chance I'd put these rods in the same category with cherry 1957 Chevys driven by older guys for reasons that aren't immediately evident. It boils down to this: If you're young now and your fly-fishing career lasts as long as you hope it will, eventually someone will point at your graphite rod and say, "You still fishin' that old thing?"

But I was never really a purist and so I cautiously tumbled for graphite when it first came out. Through a fly shop where I worked, I got a screaming deal on some J. Kennedy Fisher graphite blanks and built myself a 9-foot 5-weight and a 10-foot 6-weight. I fished the 9-footer off and on for years. I liked it, but I didn't love it and finally gave it to an old friend who was moving to Alaska and needed a grayling rod. The 10-footer never quite worked out. Like most of the 10-foot rods I've cast, it had no real reason to be longer than 9 feet, and it was a two-piece blank, so the 5-foot-long case was unwieldy. I still have it. I've tried to trade it off a few times, but no one wants it.

Through the same shop I got one of the first Sage graphite rods at cost. I think it was an 8-foot 6-weight. I remember it as having a softer, more elegant action than most graphites, which at the time were all about "speed" and "power" as if they were fly fishing's answer to muscle cars. Like most graphite rods, it was soon made obsolete by newer models, although I'm told that in certain circles those original Sage graphites are now considered modern classics. I traded that rod, but I wouldn't mind having it back now. I can't remember what I got for it, but I'd learned by then that once you put money into tackle it was best to leave it in tackle. That way you'd always have something new to play with, while cash would just slip through your fingers and be gone forever.

More recently I was given a sublime graphite rod by a filmmaker I did a small favor for. It's a 9-foot 5/6-weight that's smooth, power-ful, effortless and elegant. When I asked him what it was, he said it was just something he put together with blanks and hardware he had lying around the shop. This is one of the best graphite rods I've ever cast and I have no idea what it is. Better not break it.

To this day most of the rods I like and use are bamboo and only a few are graphite, although the graphites are gradually accumulating. Of those, most are longer rods for heavier lines—including spey rods—where I think the lighter material really shines. But that's because I came to graphite after I already had a stack of favorite bamboo rods that, for reasons of habit, sentiment or stubbornness, I wasn't about to give up. In any event, I came to understand that it doesn't matter what a fly rod is made of. What matters is how it works. It also doesn't matter if your hammer has an old-timey wood or newfangled fiberglass handle; what matters is balance and weight, which is a matter of personal preference informed by the job at hand. A light hammer is easier to swing all day, but a heavy hammer takes fewer swings and less muscle to drive a nail.

As for rod materials, I once asked the great fly caster Lefty Kreh if the then-new boron rods really cast better than graphite, as their makers claimed. He said that the best of them did, but added that the improvement was maybe 3 or 4 percent at the top end of their performance, while there probably weren't a hundred casters in the country who could get more than 50 percent of the potential out of a fly rod. So there you have it.

Most fly rods cast as well as they'll ever cast—whether it's good, bad or indifferent—with the line weight the manufacturer recommends, or at least something very close to it. Maybe a weight-forward 5 instead of a double-taper 4. But then, other rods seem so mismatched that you wonder if the line designation was a mistake. I have an 8½-foot graphite that sold years ago as a 2-weight, but that won't load at normal casting ranges with anything lighter than a double-taper 4. The silver lining there is, it's a really nice 4-weight and out here in the Rocky Mountains I don't see much use for a 2-weight anyway.

Some rod experts say that a good rod will cast a wide variety of line sizes. I think what they mean is that it can be *made* to cast with some effort, but every rod I've ever liked had a sweet spot that could only be satisfied by a very specific line size. This kind of fine-tuning may approach a universal truth about all tools. An old woodcutter once told me it didn't matter what kind of chain saw you used, but "if your chain ain't sharpened right, your kerf goes all cattywampus."

There *is* a difference between fly lines from different manufacturers, although not always as much as their claims might lead you to think. I spent a long time trying out all the fly lines I could get my hands on and then finally settled on a single make of line I liked and that I now use for almost all my fishing. (Coincidentally, it's the only line I know of that hasn't changed since the early 1970s, except that it now comes in a fancy plastic box. They've added "Classic" to the name and of course it costs more.) It's possible that I'm missing something, but this combination of habit and brand loyalty eliminates unpleasant surprises and keeps life a little simpler.

I think we each eventually settle on a handful of line weights that mirror the fishing we do and that strike some ergonomic chord. I instinctively want a 5-weight for most of my local trout fishing—it just feels right—although the length of the rod can vary from 7½ to 9 feet, depending on the water. I have a few 4-weights I also really like, but I feel that anything lighter is either impractical or a gimmick. For a heavier rod I prefer a 9-foot 8-weight, and I have some real sweethearts, including a Payne bamboo and a Loop graphite. Many good casters prefer a 7-weight and have no use for an 8, but 7-weights strike me as too much for some purposes and not enough for others. A good 6-weight, on the other hand, is like a souped-up 5-weight for larger fish, wider rivers and bigger flies. Or is all that just an excuse to have a whole bunch of fly rods?

For Spey rods I like the versatility of a 13- or 14-foot 9-weight. Lighter, shorter two-handed rods are in fashion now, but you can fish a 9-weight anywhere, including situations that involve big water, big fish and flies the size of squirrels. I went through several Spey rods before I settled on a pair of 9-weights that I like: one 13½-feet, the other 14. It would be nice if I could leave it at that, but although I own enough rods to build a picket fence around my property, I can sometimes be convinced that I need *just one more*.

In the long run, it's possible that there's no such thing as the perfect fly rod because a rod is a study in paradoxes. It has to be as long as possible but as short as necessary; sensitive but powerful; able to cast a line and play a fish (two distinctly different chores) and so on. A good fly rod would fit Aristotle's idea of virtue as falling midway between two defects, so that courage is well beyond cowardice, but somewhere short of recklessness.

Tempting as it is, I won't list all my favorite rods here, if only because it's impossible to adequately describe a fly rod in purely technical terms, so I'd end up sounding like an overbred wine connoisseur with his pinky out. I will say I sometimes have to remind myself that I love the best rods I have because I don't think about them when I'm casting them—which is precisely what makes them so good. Some of my favorites seem to defy the laws of physics as well as my own inadequacies. You could call them "effortless." Or maybe "forgiving."

There are some rods and some casters with truly weird idiosyncrasies and sometimes they find each other and live happily ever after, but for the most part I think good rods fall into a fairly narrow range. What separates a good one from a great one usually isn't some new taper or material, but a subtlety of action and balance that's recognizable but indescribable. Individual casting style has less to do with rod quality than some think, although it *is* possible not to appreciate a rod that's widely considered to be great or to love one for reasons that are more sentimental than practical.

I'll guess that I've owned somewhere in the neighborhood of a hundred fly rods at one time or another and still have around half that many, although some haven't seen the light of day in years. In any given season I might fish only eight or nine of those rods as conditions and moods dictate, and I'd be a better caster if I fished only two or three. Most of the rods I've owned were perfectly okay. Among the rest, I've loved a few and hated a few others without much reference to what they cost, what they were made of, or what anyone else thought of them.

I was a self-taught caster in the beginning and I'm afraid it still shows, especially when I'm tired or excited. (The best thing to do when your casting goes to hell is to reel in and take a ten-minute break.) I went for something like thirty years without taking a formal casting lesson because lessons weren't widely available when I was a beginner and I probably couldn't have afforded them anyway. And by the time they *were* available, I felt like I knew what I was doing. Over the years I got tips from some good casters and learned to study fishermen who seemed to know what they were doing. In time, I managed to unlearn some of my bad habits and pieced together some fundamentals: It's all about line speed, timing, smoothness, economy of motion and letting the rod do the work, even on long, windy casts. (Speaking of wind, I learned it's helpful to think of yourself as leaning against it instead of fighting it head on. If you fight it, the wind always wins.) Then, when I did finally take what was described as an "advanced casting seminar," I was embarrassed by how much it helped.

I now own some of the best fly rods I've ever cast—plus a bunch of others that I don't really know what to do with—but I'm not sure if that's helped or hurt. When it's all said and done, I'm an adequate fly caster with an option to be slightly better than most when I'm fishing a favorite rod on familiar water on a good day. But I'll probably never be as efficient or as stylish as I'd like to be. I was fishing with a friend once and we got to talking about casting during a break. I said, "I always wanted to be a pretty caster" (maybe trolling for a little compliment). He said, "Well, you're not, but you get the fly where you want it and that's what counts."

8

THE MILE

The conceit among trout fishers is that we're all such unreconstructed fanatics that when fishing possibilities dwindle over the winter we go quietly insane. In fact, some do—and not always quietly—but others seem to take the break more or less in stride and a few even think it's "good for the soul," as Nick Lyons once said, to have an off-season for rest and reflection.

   I go back and forth myself. I do go quietly insane at times, although the apparent cause is usually CNN rather than a lack of fishing. It's true that a week somewhere with a fly rod in my hand would affect a cure, but then so would the same week at home without TV or newspapers. For the most part though, I'm happy enough to think about where I've been, plan where I'll go next, tie flies, fuss with tackle and try my best to make a living.

I was doing just that toward the end of February when my friend Vince called and proposed a quickie. We'd drive up to the Miracle Mile in Wyoming, fish for two days with an overnight camp and then head home. I'd been hearing about the Mile—as it's called—for years, but had obstinately never fished it. I think I was put off by the name as much as by the crowd it's known to draw at certain times of year. "Miracle Mile" sounds more like a roadside theme park than a stretch of the North Platte River in Wyoming that's famous for good trout fishing. It's not even accurate because the stretch of river the name refers to is actually more like six miles long. (One symptom of incipient off-season insanity is that I become my high school English teacher, snidely correcting imprecise language at every opportunity.)

The weather was seasonably cold and uninviting, the forecast was for more of the same and there was no available fishing report. I jumped on the invitation with more eagerness than I thought was in me.

The drive to the river was familiar from other trips north until we peeled off the interstate at the dreary refinery town of Sinclair and started out across the Red Desert. This is a region without clear boundaries that's been variously described as hostile, inhospitable, unforgiving and haunting, but its salient feature is that there's no one there. The population density of Carbon County, Wyoming, is roughly one person for every three square miles, but that's deceptive since better than half of them live in the county seat of Rawlins and are smart enough to stay in town in the winter. Out on County Road 351, anyone at all constitutes a crowd and seeing another car amounts to traffic.

Except for a low pass through the Seminoe Mountains, this area is largely treeless, with scattered sage, sparse grasses and tough little shrubs like cedar rim thistle and bladderpod, all hanging on for dear life in what Annie Proulx called "bad dirt." Living things tend to stay low here, while rocks that stand up in the constant, sandy wind are abraded into the spooky mushroom shapes geologists call "hoodoos."

Wind is a fact of life as well as the basis for rural Wyoming humor. Mark Spragg said, "There are people here who'd like to move away, but they'd have to go outside to do it." A man living in a town that eleven souls now call home once told me, "We're losin' people. Even the wind is in a big fuckin' hurry to be somewhere else."

For long stretches of the drive there were no human artifacts except for the unpaved road we were on and the ubiquitous western barbed wire fences that Ted Leeson described as separating "a great deal of one thing from a lot more of the same." It had snowed recently, but most of the snow had blown away, leaving ominous-looking drifts across the road in the low spots. You'd normally stop and inspect drifts for depth on a road like this because it's the last place you'd want to get stuck, but there were fairly recent skidding tire tracks through the snow, so we'd put the truck in high-range four-wheel, pick up some speed on the downslope and fishtail through, postponing second thoughts until we were back on bare ground on the other side.

When we finally got down to the river, we reconnoitered for half an hour, looking at fishy-looking water and keeping an eye out without much luck for a spot to camp out of the wind. There were a few cottonwoods along the river, but not enough in any one place to make a proper shelterbelt. We picked out a long tailing pool above a bridge and gave it half an hour. There was no sign of insect or fish life, but the water was easily readable, so you could tell where the fish would be if they were there. After thirty minutes I believed that I may or may not have had a halfhearted bump to a nymph. It was the usual first act on a new river at less than the best time of year.

When we went to try another spot, the pickup wouldn't start. Vince turned the key and instead of the usual growl of a V-8 engine coming to life, there was the disheartening click that tells you there isn't enough juice to turn over the starter. This means corroded terminals if you're lucky, a dead battery if you're not.

When you're out in winter weather, the pickup is a real icon of survival: a mobile windbreak with a heater that, in a pinch, can get you the many miles to the nearest McDonald's or Motel 6. When it fails to start forty-some miles up a lonesome dirt road with no traffic, you experience what can only be called profound disappointment. We stared ahead through the windshield at sagebrush twitching in the wind. Nothing was said. When we'd driven around earlier, we'd seen a few other fishermen parked here and there along the river, but the chances of any of them happening by anytime soon seemed slim. Vince told me later he was beginning to formulate a plan, although he didn't fill me in on the details. I was simply thinking that we'd taken his truck because it was newer and more reliable than mine.

At which point our friend Corey pulled up, having recognized the truck. I stepped out of the passenger door to shake hands. Vince began digging behind the seat for the jumper cables. As it turned out, the battery terminals were pristine, as anything Vince maintains usually is, but the battery itself was eight months past its expiration date and wouldn't hold a charge. So we fished with Corey for the rest of the day because he's our friend and we like his company, because he knows the river, and because the truck would no longer start without a jump, so we had to stay close to a functioning vehicle.

For the same reason, we camped together that night in a bivouac that consisted of eight fishermen ranging in age from their early twenties to past sixty. I'm not at all sure who most of these people were except that everyone seemed to know someone else and so we'd all ended up together in a sparse grove of narrow-leaf cottonwoods that had no effect on the cold wind except to funnel it into stronger gusts.

Everyone had packed in firewood—from neatly split pine logs to construction scraps—so we got a uselessly huge bonfire going. The temperature had dropped into the low thirties even before the sun went down. After dark the wind picked up and came from a different direction every five minutes. Hunkered around the fire, you'd either get a face full of smoke and sparks or your ears would be cold even as tread melted off the soles of your boots.

Someone tossed foil-wrapped potatoes at the edge of the fire to bake. Once that suggestion had been planted, the rest of us dug out propane stoves and the usual odd assortment of camp food ranging from quick, cheap and easy to elaborate. While we were cooking supper, someone produced a battery-operated boom box. I've never cared for recorded music in camp and I rolled my eyes at Vince, but then when a vintage Bob Dylan tune came out of the thing, I softened a little.

It had turned full dark and bitterly cold by the time we'd all gotten supper taken care of and had settled in for some serious campfire sitting. Eight lawn chairs were crammed in a seamless ring around the fire pit, but it wasn't possible to either build the blaze big enough or to sit quite close enough to it. Cans of beer and a bottle of tequila appeared, and although I don't actually remember seeing a joint going around, I do recall a familiar whiff of something that wasn't wood smoke. Some trout had been caught that day, but I won't say how many in case you'd think the trip wasn't "worthwhile" in the way some understand that term.

It must have been on someone's mind because the talk turned to women earlier than it usually does in a camp full of men. "You need a woman who likes to travel and fish herself, but who doesn't always want to come along," someone said. "You know, she's gotta give you some space." We were lined up around the fire nearly in each other's laps and all nodded agreement on the need for space in relationships.

Even the youngest of these guys was old enough now to have had these things go south a few times, although why is never clear. The assumption is that these are affairs of the heart and therefore a great and tender mystery, but we're men, after all; we can work it out logically. When a lull in the conversation came, I felt an urge to say something wise befitting the thirty or forty years I had on some of these guys. But nothing came to mind except a youth filled with older men droning on as if they owned the secrets of the universe, never mind that their own lives were train wrecks. Then the moment passed and the conversation drifted off in the predictable direction of pickups, boats, fly rods and increasingly long, fire-gazing silences.

Finally one man said, apropos of nothing, "I'm like a largemouth bass: I lurk . . . and then I *pounce!*"

Someone else replied, "Damn right."

It was getting late.

I've never been much of a winter camper, although I did once spend an experimental night in a snow cave to see if it would be as cozy as some claimed. It wasn't. In other words, I don't have actual winter camping gear, but I make do by stuffing a so-called three-season sleeping bag inside a summer-weight bag and sleeping in full long johns, fleece socks, sweatshirt and wool hat. On that particular night it was stinging cold away from the fire and I reread only a page of *The Meadow* by James Galvin before I nestled in to generate a pocket of heat by burning calories. I had the tent cinched tight as a drum with rocks on top of the stakes to keep them from working loose, but the wind was still up and the rain fly flapped like a trapped condor. Even with that racket I managed to drift off before I was actually warm. I'd only gotten good and cozy hours later when I woke up in the middle of the night with an undeniable urge to pee.

For some reason, cold, windy nights in tents are when I'm most likely to have one of those luminous dreams where everything suddenly fits together. I wake up with the fleeting sense that I've been given the answer to an important question I don't remember asking and lay there in the first light trying to remember what it was. Then I get sidetracked by thoughts of coffee and a big cold-weather breakfast: as much chopped-up bacon as will fit in the pan with room left over for half a dozen eggs scrambled in and four slices of whole wheat bread scorched over the fire to approximate toast. It's calm this morning, but colder than it was last night, so frost will condense on the propane bottle before the percolator on the camp stove starts to bubble. I can picture it all vividly. Now all I have to do is pry myself out of my warm spot and make it happen.

Corey is already up and a little too cheerful as I force my fingers to work enough to get the coffee started. He asks if I heard the great horned owl last night, and I say I did but don't add that I thought it was part of the dream. A snore comes from one of the tents, and I think we're the only two awake until I glance downstream and see one of the younger guys at a bend pool landing what looks like a good-sized trout. I'm deeply impressed but not exactly envious. For some, winter fishing is the kind of extreme sport that separates the men from the boys, as they used to say. But then for others it's a more pensive enterprise where the fire and the coffeepot compete on equal footing with the river.

When our gonzo companion sees activity in camp, he trudges back, and we learn that he got that trout and one other—both rainbows—on a Girdle Bug. I ask if he knows the origin of that fly's name and he doesn't. I explain that the rubber legs on the first ones were made from elastic strips salvaged from discarded girdles. He nods politely. It's possible he's not that into fly-tying trivia, or maybe he's heard of girdles but is too young to have ever actually seen one, let alone tried to wrestle one off his date in the backseat of a 1962 Ford Fairlane.

During this short conversation the guy has wolfed down a granola bar and chugged a big cup of coffee. Then he opens a fly box, gives me a neatly tied brown Girdle Bug and walks back toward the river. Bottom-line types in the fly tackle industry worry about the future of the sport, but it seems to me there's an endless supply of these young fly casters who, as far as the ruling class is concerned, fish and drink too much, work too little, are at perpetual loose ends about jobs and girlfriends, but always have a fishing trip in the works. Few of them earn enough to be valuable customers now, but that will likely change because they're genetically programmed for success in the twenty-first century. By that I mean they're comfortable with technology, but they're not in love with it and recognize its limitations. They work hard when they work, they tend to be nonpolitical without being ignorant to the point of negligence and they take things no more seriously than they need to be taken.

Even with the provocation of a couple of trout being caught, it takes some of us another hour to get fed, suited up and on the water. Corey and I planned to air out our spey rods that day. We'd swing weighted streamers through the big runs, and if that didn't work we'd rest the water and come back with nymphs. I'd never fished a nymph with a spey rod, but I'd heard about it and wanted to try it. If nothing else, the reach of a 13½-foot rod would be a tremendous advantage. The fishing had been slow, but not dead, and I had big plans for that Girdle Bug.

In the mean time, Vince had crawled out of his tent blinking and yawning and I'd all but finished the coffee, so I poured him the dregs and started a fresh pot. I'd come to fish and I'd get around to it eventually, but the real reason for the trip was simply to get out of the house in the winter and there I was, so there was no rush.

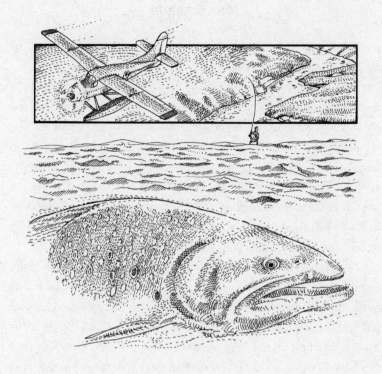

9

TREE RIVER

The weather was deteriorating the morning we flew to the Tree River. The vintage de Havilland Otter—loaded with nine fishermen, two guides and a breathtaking pile of fishing tackle—cruised at an altitude of around 100 feet, midway between stark tundra and a low, drizzling overcast. The air was unstable, and although I've had bumpier trips than this one in floatplanes, there was still the sense of taking a long ride in a defective elevator. I'd had a big breakfast before leaving camp—pancakes, eggs, sausages and at least a quart of coffee—and although I wasn't exactly queasy, I did notice that the airsick bag compartment was empty.

Back at the dock, the pilot, Wes, had joked us out of any misgivings we might have had about the weather. After running down a few basic safety procedures, he added, "And remember, whatever else happens, save the pilot at any cost," inducing the kind of nervous laughter that doesn't exactly make you brave, but at least helps you keep breakfast down. Although I'd met Wes only the day before, I'd already come to know him as one of those guys who puts a fresh cigar in his mouth every morning, but never quite gets around to smoking it. He seemed like a man you could trust.

I'm not normally a white-knuckle flier and I'm actually more comfortable in small planes than in big ones, even though the odds lean in the other direction. But as pleasant as it was to fly low and look for wildlife, I couldn't help remembering the adage that altitude is the bush pilot's best friend because the higher you are, the more time you have to work out any problems that might come up. On the other hand, I'd been hoping to see musk ox and I did. From the air they look like hair balls, and if they weren't running, you wouldn't be able to tell one end from the other.

I was going to this particular river in the Canadian Arctic for the simple reason that Plummer's Great Bear Lake Lodge, which operates the only fishing camp there, blatantly advertises it as "The best arctic char river in the world." Of course, extravagant claims are common in the outfitting business and some of them strain credulity, but this one was more verifiable than most. The all-tackle world-record Arctic char—thirty-two pounds, nine ounces—was caught in the Tree River in 1981, and since the early 1990s the river has accounted for every fly-rod tippet-class record between 4- and 20-pound test. A world record could be a fluke (most are, almost by definition), but six other record-book fish in the space of a decade and a half seemed pretty convincing.

I wasn't after a record myself and frankly have some doubts about that whole enterprise. At its best, maximum fish size is of some interest to scientists as well as fishermen and establishing a tippet-class record amounts to nothing more than some harmless competitive bragging. But at its worst, I've seen people lose fish after fish trying to land them on tackle that was too light for the job or, worse yet, get thoroughly pissed off at what should have been the catch of a lifetime because it fell two ounces short of going down in history.

So in my self-consciously modest way, I was just hoping to catch a few, and since these were sea-run fish, I assumed they'd be bigger and tougher than the landlocked char I'd caught in Alaska and Labrador. Of course, all those records were tantalizing, but they weren't a guarantee of success, by any means. Anyone who's gone after anadromous fish that have run into freshwater rivers to spawn understands that, like salmon and steelhead, they'll bite or not for reasons of their own.

The Tree River is in the Kitikmeot region of the Inuit-governed territory of Nunavut—an enormous, sparsely inhabited area lying north of Manitoba and Saskatchewan, east of the Northwest Territories and west of Baffin Bay. If Nunavut isn't on your map of Canada, it's because your map was printed prior to 1999 when the territory was carved out of the old Northwest Territories to settle ongoing Inuit land claims. Nunavut covers 777,000 square miles, or 20 percent of the Canadian landmass. Estimates of its population usually come in at around 30,000—mostly native people who can trace their ancestry back to the last ice age. The way we see it, almost all of it is uninhabited, although an Inuit fisherman might point out that you can "inhabit" a place without stringing barbed wire and posting NO TRESPASSING" signs.

When I first went to the Northwest Territories to fish in the 1970s, talks with the Canadian government about an Inuit homeland were just beginning. The prevailing opinion among guides and fishermen in the camp was that this was a doomed idealistic exercise. I reluctantly agreed—if only because in America, with our appalling history in those matters, it would have been—so I was especially delighted to come back twenty-some years later and shell out $15.75 Canadian for an official Nunavut fishing license.

The Tree River camp itself lies roughly 150 miles north of the Arctic Circle and 3 miles upriver (that is, south) of the Arctic Ocean at Amundsen Bay. Parts of the riverbank are choked with nearly impenetrable knee-high wolf willow, but the country for a thousand square miles around is tundra where the diversity of plants is astonishing, but nothing grows much higher than the sole of a boot. No one in camp knew for sure why it was called the Tree River, but the best guess was that it was named ironically by Europeans vainly searching for firewood a hundred miles from the nearest tree.

On a normal fly-out to the river from the main lodge at Great Bear Lake, you get an afternoon and a morning of fishing with an overnight in a snug little fisherman's hooch with plywood walls, a canvas roof and a cranky oil heater. It may be possible to wangle another full day if the next group in is short a man or to luck into one if the weather turns sour and the Otter can't fly. But even if you can stretch it, there's the knowledge that cracking this new fishery could take more time than you have. You firmly believe that once you get the right corner worked loose you can peel the whole thing open, but on previous trips to other rivers that's taken the better part of a week or more, much of it spent waiting for the weather or the fish's mood to change. Still, you remind yourself that the trick to fishing well is not to rush, because hurrying only makes things go wrong.

My guide, Craig Blackie, ferried me across the river in one of the boats they keep above the first rapids for that purpose and hiked me a mile upriver on a muddy trail to an unimpressive-looking notch in the bank. It was a small, bumpy side current not much bigger than a couple of parking spaces lying alongside a dangerous-looking rip.

I'm not good at judging stream flow on big water, but this was clearly in the thousands of cubic feet per second, and along this bank it was tipped and squeezed into a torrent. It reminded me of the speeding freight trains I liked to watch as a kid and of my parents telling me I'd be sucked under the wheels if I got too close.

It was a tricky drift in conflicting currents and there were jumbled rocks on the bottom that snagged my weighted streamer twice in a dozen casts. Then there was a thump I thought was another rock until it shook its head ponderously. The fish bulldogged in the side current for a minute or so, just long enough for me to innocently think I might be able to land it there. Then it rolled out into the white water and took me far into the backing in a matter of seconds. I felt as if I'd foul-hooked a piano.

After one failed try where the current was still too fast, we finally got it to the net in a narrow slick ten minutes later and a hundred yards downstream. It was a hen about thirty-five inches long that Blackie guessed at thirteen pounds. I was delighted to have landed her, but I was even happier about getting my fly line back. I'd brought a spare, but it was an hour's round-trip walk away, back in camp.

Farther upstream we fished the Presidential Pool, named for the elder President Bush, who'd fished it some years ago. This was the most luxurious pool I saw on the Tree, a big, brawling river where most of the good reachable holding water is small enough to be fished out while one stands in one spot. It was seventy-five or eighty yards long and channeled roughly a third of the river's volume into a swift current tight to the near bank with a slower slick farther out. The successful cast was a long reach to the head of the slick with a hard upstream mend and a high-stick swing designed to keep the line from bellying. It was a long cast and a hard drift, but I managed it and felt like I was on my game, although it would be just as true to say that the fish were biting. I was fishing a 13½-foot 9-weight spey rod with a short sinking tip, a stubby fifteen-pound leader, several hundred yards of backing and a size 1/0 white streamer. Through trial and error, the guides have arrived at white as the hands-down favorite fly color.

The char weren't exactly stacked in this run, but now and then we'd see a wide back roll or, if the chromy light was just right, the flash of a long orange belly under the surface. When hooked, the fish fought hard—occasionally jumping, though mostly bulldogging with their heads down—but for some reason they didn't want to leave the pool. These were strong, heavy fish, and if any of them had wanted to head for the main river and spool me, there wouldn't have been much I could have done about it, although God knows I'd have tried.

That evening we all met for supper at the lodge, a garage-sized frame building consisting of a kitchen and three picnic tables in one room. Some of us had caught fish and others hadn't: the oldest story in the book. There were both fly and gear fishermen in camp and neither method had definitively beaten out the other. A guide named Trevor said the fishing had been okay but not as good as it *can* be, so it had all come down to the usual ineffable confluence of skill and luck, or what the old-timers used to call "holding your mouth right."

That night I settled into my shack—a word I use affectionately— by stripping off my wet clothes and hanging them to dry around the heater. (My twelve-year-old rain slicker had chosen this trip to start leaking at the shoulder seams.) There was one small window, four cots, a single straight-backed chair, a shaving mirror the size of a book, a wash pan, assorted coat hooks, a clothesline stretched in the low roof peak, a galvanized bucket on the stove for warm, if not actually hot, water and a single bare lightbulb powered by a generator. The river was clearly audible and so was the pattering of rain on the canvas roof. It was the kind of place that would be rustically cozy for a few nights, but that after a month could open the door to suicide if you were alone, or murder if you had roommates.

This was the third week in August with the tundra turning to autumn colors, caribou migrating south and a full three or four hours of gray dusk that passed for night. The season had started a scant five weeks earlier, and at the end of that week they'd be closing the camp for the year. I sat on a cot and scrolled through my digital camera looking at the photos Blackie had taken of the fish I'd landed that day. Guides get good at taking hero shots of clients with unfamiliar cameras and these were typically good. But with the physical memory still fresh, they looked like what they were: passable proof for the folks back home, but poor copies of the real thing displayed on a two-inch screen. It was still raining, but not very hard. The last thing I did before crawling into the sleeping bag was to put my spare spey line in my pack for tomorrow.

It has always amazed me how quickly you fall into the rhythms of a strange fishing camp, although it's true there's not much else to do. The handwritten daily schedule posted in my shack said it all:

7:30 breakfast.
Fish.
7:30 supper.

The weather had cleared a little by the next day. That is, it was still chilly and cloudy, but it wasn't raining quite as much. In the better part of twelve hours of fishing I landed one small lake trout, got a hard pull from a char, but didn't sink the hook and broke a ferrule on my spey rod going for a long cast. This was pure operator error. A spey cast generates more than enough torque to work the ferrules loose, and if you don't remember to periodically reseat them, a break is inevitable. Blackie looked at me with an expression of expectant horror, possibly anticipating a tantrum, but I've learned that the proper response to breaking a rod is simply to congratulate yourself for bringing a spare. It was coming up on suppertime and we were within sight of camp. It couldn't have happened at a better time or place.

Just above camp on the way back, we waded through the flock of willow ptarmigan that had taken up residence there. Ptarmigan never seem like the sharpest tools in the shed and these had become camp pets. We could have easily caught one in a landing net as they waddled ahead of us with all the dignity of barnyard chickens. I examined some shed flank feathers that would have made beautiful soft hackles and asked if these birds were as delicious as the smaller white-tailed ptarmigan we have back in Colorado. I do consider myself a bird-watcher, but I stand out in the usual crowd. While others are authoritatively discussing habitat preferences and migration patterns, I'm more likely to raise eyebrows by contributing fly-tying tips and recipes.

The plan for the next morning was to slip in a few hours of fishing and then hotfoot it back to camp to meet the plane back to Great Bear Lake. But by dawn the thick clouds and steady rain had socked back in and the word by shortwave was that the Otter was grounded. We were told to take our time and wander back around lunchtime to see how the weather was shaping up. I got two more char that morning: a colored-up male that looked like a brook trout in the clown suit and a fifteen-pound female. I won't try to describe the peculiar combination of olives, golds, oranges, pinks, pale blues and whites on a spawning Arctic char except to say that all fish are beautiful in their own way, but some, like these, are what a photographer friend calls "swimming jewelry."

When Blackie and I moseyed back into camp a little after noon, everyone was already assembled out front with duffels and rod cases. Word from the lodge was that the weather was clearing from the south and the plane was on its way. I just had time to pack my gear and wolf down a bowl of stew before Wes came in low and circled to land on the river.

We flew above the clouds for half an hour, but Wes is an inveterate sightseer, so as soon as we came out into the clear, we dropped back down to a hundred feet and for mile after mile I watched caribou strung out over the tundra in singles, twos and threes. Somewhere in there we crossed from Nunavut to the Northwest Territories, but there'd be no way to tell either from the air or from the ground. (It's not that the idea of ownership is unknown here, it just operates on more of an honor system than most of us are used to.) In fact, there are moments in the far north when you feel that you've fallen through time and are nowhere at all in the usual geopolitical sense. The only thing that suggests otherwise is the fishing license in your pocket.

10

OREGON

A moment comes on some fishing trips—maybe sooner, maybe later—when you begin to wonder what you've gotten yourself into. Never mind that it had been raining hard for weeks on the Oregon coast and that the rivers we intended to fish were swollen and dark. Steelhead fishing is stingy with straight answers, but one way this can go is that a flush of high water in March brings steelhead out of the salt, and when the rivers begin to drop—as they must eventually—they're stiff with bright, grabby fish. Or not, but that's one way it can happen.

More to the point, it seems ridiculous on its face to call a trip on account of rain in a region that gets enough of the stuff to support a temperate rain forest. When you live in semiarid northern Colorado, a climate this wet seems pleasantly exotic. You picture a version of the tropics with all the green lushness, but without the oppressive heat or the sunburned fun hogs. And anyway, it has rained harder there. One year there was so much rain the salmon couldn't pick the rivers out of the general deluge, so they just swam across Highway 101 and into the flooded pastures around the Tillamook Cheese Factory.

My flight out was uneventful in the modern sense that being frisked by a stranger is now standard procedure. As usual, some fellow passengers spotted me as a fisherman and asked about my trip. I don't actually wear a badge that says FISHERMAN, but I'm carrying a rod tube and wearing the sweat-stained Filson packer that my friend Ann Ripley calls "that dreadful hat," so I'm rarely mistaken for a guy on his way to a corporate board meeting.

I'd missed that morning's exchange of phone calls between my fishing partners. It seems they were rethinking the trip because of even heavier rain than expected, a grim forecast and rivers rising toward flood stage. The way I heard it later, they were exchanging sentiments like, "Dude, it's not looking good," while stopping just short of actually pulling the plug.

For that matter, I caught only snatches of the breaking news from Japan of a terrible earthquake and tsunami that had killed thousands and severely damaged several reactors at the Fukushima Daiichi Nuclear Power Plant. I may have experienced compassion fatigue. That is, the disaster seemed remote, and I was busy retrieving my duffel in Portland, renting a car, threading my way through city traffic and then heading west through the rain. I was just happy to be on the ground and going fishing.

The first I heard about tsunami warnings for the Oregon coast was from one of those lighted highway signs that usually warn of road conditions. I thought about stopping, but the sign hadn't said to turn back and there were other cars going in the same direction, most with Oregon plates. I thought these locals must know the score. Then it occurred to me that that's what every lemming in the pack must think.

At a gas station in Garibaldi, a guy said the tsunami had already hit farther south, causing plenty of damage, although less than had been feared. "Course, there can be more than one wave," he added, "but I wouldn't sweat the tsunami, I'd sweat the plume of radioactivity on its way from Japan."

I was the first to arrive at our rented cabin. As per the landlady's instructions, I worked the combination on the cellar hatch, ducked in to turn on the electricity and get the key from under a tin can, and then let myself in the front door. There was moss growing on the welcome mat. The firewood stacked on the covered porch was technically out of the weather, but it was visibly damp.

I knew that before a tsunami hits, the sea recedes, giving the fleet of foot time to dash for higher ground, so I peeked out at Tillamook Bay through the window over the kitchen sink. Except for being out of focus through the pouring rain, it looked normal. Then again, I'd seen it for the first time only an hour and a half earlier, so didn't really know how it was *supposed* to look. And of course there was no way to tell if the stiff breeze off the Pacific carried an invisible freight of radioactivity. At times like these it's worth reminding yourself that every step we take, even on a trip from the couch to the refrigerator, is a journey through time into the unknown. The only way to be sure how a fishing trip will turn out is to not go, but the regret that can dog that decision is the kind that breaks spirits and ruins lives.

When my writer friend Scott Sadil pulled in that afternoon, he filled me in on the talk of canceling the trip. There'd been serious dithering right up until the moment they realized I was already on the plane, at which point they'd decided they might as well soldier on. Scott was grinning as he told me this, but then writers have a unique perspective on these things. Sometimes the disastrous trip makes for a better story than the one where everything goes right.

I'd managed to get a smoky fire going in the stove using damp wood from the porch, but along with the groceries, Scott had brought a load of bone-dry oak and cedar that would come in real handy. I always get a rush of confidence when a fishing partner reads the conditions right and comes prepared. I think, It's gonna be okay; at least some of us know what they're doing.

When Rob Russell pulled in after dark towing his drift boat, he was all smiles and confidence. Rob has since come in out of the cold with a job selling fishing books, but he was once a steelhead guide and still exudes the kind of optimism that repels doubt the way a tight shake roof sheds rain. We were three guys going fishing in a flooded river in the rain. What could go wrong? Scott and I had been lounging and talking, but suddenly there was activity. Dinner was rustled up, the coffeepot was primed for the next morning, and there were fly boxes to be picked through, leaders to be tied and drags to be adjusted.

The river we launched on the next morning was bank-full and opaquely green, like thin pea soup. It looked pretty good. A little higher and faster than you might like, but still with defined runs where steelhead could lie up. We fished heavy tips and big, weighted flies according to the common wisdom, but Rob didn't think I was getting deep enough in the heavy current with my type-8 sink tip. He let me fish for a while, but finally couldn't stand it any longer and handed me an old Burkheimer rod loaded with a 550-grain Skagit head, a two-foot cheater, ten feet of T-14 sink tip and a four-inch-long Intruder fly with big lead eyes. I'm not much of a Skagit caster, but after a few false starts, I was lobbing this depth charge across the river and ticking gravel in the tailouts. I was feeling the surge of conviction you get when you believe you're in the zone and was, incidentally, rethinking my entire spey casting program.

Not long afterward I hooked a sea-run cutthroat—a nice fifteen-incher, but still a disappointment. It was a momentary heart-stopper, but the strike was light and hesitant and I knew it wasn't a steelhead even as I was tightening up. When you're fishing deep, the take of a steelhead feels like the smooth, deliberate motion of someone lifting a watermelon into a shopping cart. Even before you set the hook, you get an intimation of weight and strength.

When we got off the water that afternoon, we went to look at another nearby river. It was pretty well blown out, but we each made obligatory passes through the one run that still held its shape.

On the way back to the cabin, we stopped at a place on the bay for a few dozen oysters fresh from the boat. It had been breezy on the river, but out here in the open there was a thirty-knot wind, white-caps on the water and pulsing sheets of horizontal rain. The bay was churned up brown, but we could see the greenish plume of current from the river we'd been fishing extending for thousands of yards. It was easy to imagine steelhead coming in from the North Pacific, sniffing out the first scent of their home river and nosing deliberately up the familiar-smelling current.

At the door of the oyster joint, I remembered a childhood filled with women saying, "Don't you track mud in my kitchen!" and tried to shake off and dry my feet. But the guy behind the counter waved us in past the more or less permanent CAUTION, WET FLOOR sign. The oysters were raw, cold, slimy, and salty with a dash of Tabasco. Like winter steelheading, they're an acquired taste.

At the cabin we got a fire going in the stove, hung our waders and rain gear around it to dry and tossed the rest of the clothes we'd been wearing in the dryer. This was the first time all day that I realized I was soaked nearly to the skin. I'd just gotten used to it, the same way a frog sitting in a pond no longer notices that his ass is wet.

Scott had an errand the next morning. He had to drive an hour south to give a presentation at the Sitka Center for Art and Ecology, where he was ensconced in the writer-in-residence program. He said that when he was awarded this honor, they probably hadn't expected him to check in to his secluded cottage and then immediately leave to go fishing. On the other hand, they knew what kind of books he wrote, so they couldn't have been completely surprised. He said that so far no one had batted an eye, but if it came up, he'd say he was doing research for a story, which would be just true enough.

While Scott was gone, Rob and I did some wade fishing in the same water we'd floated the day before. The river was high and off-color, but the runs still looked good and I thought it was only a matter of time. I kept picturing a big, bright steelhead fresh from the ocean charging around in the confines of the river like a bull in a china shop attached to a ten-pound leader, but no dice.

We drove upstream on a logging road to look at some water above the first put-in. The river was narrower up there and most of the runs we looked at were flowing too high and fast. One looked marginally fishable, but there were already two guys parked there stringing up spey rods.

Farther upstream we walked out on a one-lane bridge to look at a beautiful pool. There was a deep slot on the far side and a long sloping tailout. You'd have to swing the whole thing from one spot on a short gravel bar, but it was doable. After I'd looked at swollen rivers for a day and a half, this was as pretty a pool as I could remember seeing. Even the color of the water was that smoky grayish jade I think of as "steelhead green." The same kind of water a client of Rob's once thought looked like toxic sludge.

We were standing there hoping to spot a steelhead holding in the tail when four guys paddling brightly colored plastic kayaks came under the bridge and headed into the pool. We cringed, but they cut to the inside to set up for the next rapids and missed the sweet spot by thirty feet.

Rob fished the run a little more cleanly than I did, but we both managed to swing flies through all the good holding water and right into the soft spot at the tailout where I fully expected a pull. I understood that from there a single flick of the tail would take a steelhead into the rapids and there'd be nothing I could do about it. I remembered a friend telling me he'd hooked a steelhead on a tributary of the Skeena in British Columbia that took him so far and fast around the next bend that when the fish broke off, his backing was stretched across dry land.

But again, no dice. Maybe the fish were there, but they were sulking. Or maybe they hadn't made it this far upriver in the high water.

We waded off the gravel bar and climbed back up to the truck. Rain was falling outright on the river's surface, but under the canopy of trees it was more of a fine spray punctuated by steady drips. We were waist-deep in ferns, and the crowns of the massive western red cedar and Sitka spruce trees were out of sight in the low ceiling.

Scott got back a little after noon. He said he'd talked a little about writing and fishing, tied a simple Green Butt Skunk—which had amazed the audience at the Center—then made his escape and headed back to the river. That first afternoon at the cabin Scott had said it was odd for a writer who thinks of himself as a journeyman to be thrust into the company of people who were encouraged to think of themselves as Artists. I quoted Richard Russo to the effect that art is just "solid craft with a dash of style." (Actually, he said "maybe" that's what it is, leaving himself some wiggle room.) Scott agreed that it was best simply to do what you do and let it stand. Whether or not you're an artist is something other people get to decide. What the artist himself thinks is immaterial.

There was still time for an afternoon float and we launched on an empty river. If other boats had gotten out ahead of us, there'd still be trailers at the put-in, but the parking lot was vacant. It looked as though everyone had bailed except those two diehards on the logging road that morning. We waded some runs, but swung most from the boat, if only because the river had come up and there was no place left to stand.

We ended up anchored in a good run one long bend upstream from the takeout, trading turns swinging from the bow. Hope remained high. If tide fish were in, this is where they'd be and there was no earthly reason why one of us shouldn't hook one. I'm far from adept at this, but I know enough to get by and I'm comforted by the knowledge that although a good steelheader owns many skills that serve him well over the long haul, he'll sometimes be out-fished by a persistent klutz.

That's what I was thinking when a squall hit. We heard and saw it coming upstream for a few seconds: a roaring sound, trees leaning dangerously and an opaque wall of water I thought was rain and Rob later said was a cloud of spray boiling off the river. We just had time to grab the spare rods and hang on before this thing spun the boat around on the anchor rope, pushed boat and anchor several yards upstream and slammed us against a high bank. We came within inches of swamping; the bank side oar shot out of its lock and into the river and the temperature dropped thirty degrees.

It lasted a few minutes and then things went back to normal except that the rain-spattered river was now littered with good-sized tree branches. Scott asked, "What the fuck was that?" but there was no answer. Rob was busy putting the spare oar together so we could catch up to the one we lost before the takeout. I thought "microburst," but didn't say it out loud because it was just a word I'd heard somewhere in connection with weather.

Rob left after dark that evening in order to make the long drive home in time for work the next morning, and Scott went outside to check in with the guide we had booked for the next few days. Cellphone reception on the coast is worse than spotty, but Scott had discovered that if you stood in the rain on the bottom porch step you could get a signal.

I was fussing with the cranky flue on the stove when Scott came back in and said, "The guide's not coming."

"What?"

"He's not coming. He said he checked the weather forecast and the flow and it's pointless."

"Really?"

We decided to put in one more day on our own. No telling why except that there's something resembling a work ethic in operation here. Or maybe it's just the good-natured stubbornness I like to think of as uniquely American whereby no one wants to be the first to call it quits. Not that there's anything heroic about fishing. Remember that when a nonangler sees one of us casting in the rain, his likely thought is, Now there's a guy with nothing better to do. Still, I couldn't help thinking how sweet it would be to land a steelhead after the guide had said it was no use. You wouldn't be mean about it, but you *would* e-mail him a grip-and-grin shot of a stupendous chromer with the message "Sorry you couldn't make it."

We ended the next day standing on the bridge where Rob and I had seen the kayakers. We'd spent hours driving up the river, casting halfheartedly to some runs and simply looking at others that would have been beautiful at half their current flow. At some point we stopped carrying our rods down to the river, a sure sign that we'd quit fishing and were now just sightseeing. Of course, the run Rob and I had fished a little over twenty-four hours ago was now a shapeless torrent. I could pick out where the tailout and the handy gravel bar had been, but there was now no sign of them.

As we stood on the bridge in the rain, possibly looking a little dejected, a rusty pickup pulled up behind us and stopped. The driver rolled down his window and asked, "How's the fishin'?" We turned to reply, but then saw that he was wearing the lopsided grin peculiar to fishermen who already know the answer to that question.

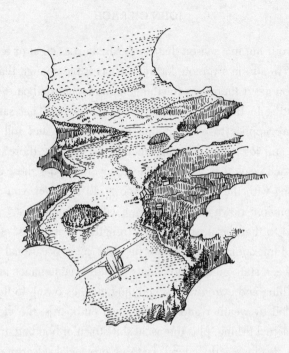

11

LODGES

As commercial enterprises, fishing lodges are rarely big moneymakers, which is one of the reasons the turnover and mortality rates are so high. The editor of a sporting magazine once told me it's not all that unusual for him to assign a destination story on a lodge only to have the place change owners or close before the article runs. Think about it: you're operating what amounts to a hotel, a restaurant, a guide service, a travel agency, a small airline, a modest navy and occasional medical evacuation unit, and you sometimes have to make your nut in a season that can be as short as eight or ten weeks.

You're also in a remote location inaccessible enough that, by the time you get it there, gas for the generators and outboards can end up costing in the neighborhood of $25 a gallon. That same price structure applies to every pound of hamburger and roll of toilet paper, and logistics are a nightmare. Chances are there's a single flight each week that can bring in whatever supplies there are room for along with the next group of sports. In between, you can't just send someone down to the store for a gallon of milk.

Add to that the needs, wants, strengths, weaknesses, eccentricities and unexamined fantasies of the fishermen, occasional tiffs with or between staff, guides and clients, endless maintenance and repair of anything and everything, scheduling glitches owing to floatplanes grounded by weather and broken-down outboards, the vicissitudes of the actual fishing, plus the usual shit-storm of bonding, insurance, various dealings with federal, state or provincial governments and/ or tribal councils and a bunch of other things I haven't thought of because it's not my job. (My job at a fishing lodge consists largely of showing up on time for breakfast.) It no longer surprises me when things go wrong at fishing lodges. What surprises me is that things so often go right.

The most well-adjusted lodge owner I know once told me that he'd made his money elsewhere (not an unlimited amount, but enough), that he loved spending his summers in the far north among fishermen, guides and bush pilots and, although he wasn't against turning a profit, all he really needed to do was break even. Most years he did. We were sitting up late talking in one of the cabins at the lodge. I glanced at my watch and mentioned that the generator would be turned off in five minutes and the lights would go out. He smiled and said, "I own the place; the lights go out when I say they do." Then he added, "Or when the generator breaks down."

I've met a few lodge owners who were all about business plans, projected earnings and inane policy statements about "reconceptualizing the paradigm," but the happiest and, oddly enough, many of the most successful, seemed to do it simply for love and a modest livelihood. I knew a man in Alaska who went there initially to hunt brown bears. He eventually killed one and decided he never wanted to do it again, but by then he'd fallen in love with the region and in the fullness of time ended up owning a fishing lodge where the guides weren't allowed to carry firearms and the fishermen were required to sign liability waivers. He said he went into the lodge business with his eyes open, understanding that if he wanted to get rich he should do something else. One night every week he'd stand gravely at the head of the table after dinner and recite Robert W. Service poems from memory. ("There are strange things done in the midnight sun / By the men who moil for gold" and so on.) Meanwhile, the same midnight sun would shine through the window casting amber light on that moldering old bearskin.

I enjoy and appreciate fishing lodges, but not everyone does. Balls-to-the-wall types may see regular mealtimes and other necessary regimentation as a waste of valuable fishing time. Self-styled experts sometimes chafe at having guides tell them where to go and what to do, although most of us would do well to let go of old certainties and learn. Do-it-yourselfers used to handling things on their own are sometimes uncomfortable being waited on. And even at a real wilderness outfit, some adventurers can feel confined to water they think has been fished too hard by too many others before them. A precious few of these folks will end up mounting their own expeditions, but for most of us that's beyond the practical limit. That's why there are lodges.

Every fishing lodge is different, but most visits begin the same way. You step off the floatplane onto the dock, shake the hands of the camp manager and guides and, if you're smart, make real sure all your gear is unloaded. Then you schlep your luggage to your room or cabin and assemble in the lodge for the short orientation meeting. Here you get the lowdown, which can be simple or complicated, depending on where you are.

At a lodge in Labrador that's known for its catch-and-release fishing for large brook trout, the owner said, "There are only two hard-and-fast rules here: One, no brook trout will be killed. Ever. And two, if your guide tells you to do something, do it. We can argue about it later." Up till then it had all been hot coffee and good-natured hospitality, but there was a change in tone that suggested these two items went right to the heart of the matter.

Sure enough, a few days later we were two hours from the lodge across a big lake fishing a river outlet; three of us in an eighteen-foot flat-stern canoe with a ten-horse outboard. The fishing was good and the only reason I noticed that the wind had stiffened and changed direction was that the mosquitoes abruptly stopped pestering me. But then our guide appeared at my shoulder and said, "Reel in, we gotta go."

It took ten minutes to hustle back to the outlet where the canoe was beached, and before we even got there, we could feel the new chill in the air and see whitecaps building on the lake. The crowns of spruce trees bobbed in the wind and the pearl-colored overcast darkened to a soggy gunmetal gray. We motored up the windward shore, staying in the shelter of the trees until we got directly upwind of the lodge. Then we turned and made the run across the lake. By then the wind had really picked up, the air had turned cold and big rain drops hit the backs of our slickers like gravel fired from a slingshot. A hundred yards off shore we were in serious rollers.

A lesser boatman would have just made a dash for it, but our guy was smart enough to feather the outboard as we rose lazily on the big swells and then gun it into the troughs so we didn't fatally ship water over the stern. I had a death grip on the gunnels of the canoe, as if that might help. This seemed to be going okay, but it was easy to see how that could change. As we neared the camp, we spotted the entire staff waiting for us on the dock. The owner was watching through binoculars. Two guides were in an aluminum dory with the motor idling, ready to come for us if it looked like we wouldn't make it.

But we did make it and the head cook, a sweet woman named Frances, herded us over to the lodge for hot coffee and an embarrassing amount of fussing. Our own mothers wouldn't have been any more worried about us or any more relieved that we were back safe.

That storm trapped us in our cabin for the next two and a half days. There was horizontal rain, gale-force winds, and it was cold enough for a daytime fire in the woodstove. Boredom closed in, but every time I started to mourn the fishing I'd left, I reminded myself of the two alternatives to coming in when we did: We could have waited and tried to cross the lake in even rougher seas and most likely drowned, or we could have stayed where we were to spend the next sixty hours out in the spectacular havoc of one of the worst storms I've ever seen with no provisions and no shelter.

The moral is, if your guide tells you to do something, do it. On subsequent trips to that lodge, I've sat through the same speech nodding wisely, now the old hand who knows the score.

This business of camp rules is a matter of style and every lodge handles it differently. Some, like the guy in Labrador, keep it simple. Others list everything that could possibly go wrong and either confuse you or scare you to death. A guy at a bass camp in south Texas just said, "Watch where you step. Everything down here will stick you, sting you or bite you and most of it's poison." On the other hand, I was once at a place in New Mexico where the manager, a tall man in a cowboy hat and snap-button shirt, grinned widely, slapped me on the back and said, "There's only one rule here, and that's that *there are no rules.*"

I understood this to be hyperbole, and in fact I learned from the head guide that earlier that year this guy had booted a famous movie star who couldn't, or wouldn't, control his two large, troublesome dogs. Angry words were spoken, something to the effect of "I don't give a shit who you are. I want you out of here now." Sometimes the biggest glad-handers turn out to be the ones with the shortest fuses.

Now and then, there are rules you abide by without ever knowing it. At a lodge in Alaska, the head cook—who also happened to be the owner's wife—finally got tired of fishermen coming in early on slow or stormy days to hang around asking for coffee, wanting to talk and otherwise getting in the way while she prepared her labor-intensive meals. So one day she sat the guides down and said, "I don't care how bad the fishing or the weather is, I want you to keep these people on the water and out of my kitchen until dinnertime." Later that season a fisherman was heard to say, with undisguised admiration, "Man, these guides are gung ho. They won't come in no matter what."

One thing that never changes, though, is the moment you step off the floatplane or boat onto the dock and into the gaze of the assembled guides who have come to size you up. I've seen people strut and preen and bluster, but it's pointless. These guys will know all they need to about you in the first ten minutes on the water. The only thing you can say to a guide that will impress him is, "I've never fished here before. I'll appreciate any help you can give me."

Of course, tipping is mandatory except in the kind of extreme circumstances that I've heard horror stories about but have never actually experienced. How much is up to you, your wallet and your conscience, but an enormous fish is worth a little extra. So is heroic effort, whether it results in fish or not.

Some lodges put their tips into a kitty to be divvied up later, which begs a couple of questions: Do the cook and the camp manager get the same cut as the guides? *Should* they get the same cut? When I think my guide has gone above and beyond, I'll put some money in the pot, then get the guy alone and slip him an extra hundred. I tip as much as I can. More often than not it doesn't seem like enough.

Every lodge eventually develops its own subculture, which is the result of an initial plan that's been gradually informed and sometimes *de*formed by the people who run the outfit, as well as the realities of water, weather and fish. An Atlantic salmon or steelhead lodge where two or three fish can make for a bang-up week will naturally have a different sensibility than a place with five species of Pacific salmon where catches of commercial proportions aren't unheard of.

Part of lodge culture has to do with what we'd now call the level of service. Some outfits go heavy on the sumptuous accommodations and leisurely gourmet meals on the correct assumption that those are the only things they can control, while most of the things that can go wrong with the fishing are what an insurance agent would call "acts of God." I was once at a place where the salmon run was canceled when a nearby volcano belched tons of evil-smelling sulfurous sludge into the river. Not much anyone could do about that.

As long as the fishing is good, I have nothing against palatial lodges with vaulted ceilings, deer-antler chandeliers and five-course meals, and I know there are some who really enjoy that sort of thing. I once met a man at a fancy lodge who said, "I know it's a little over the top, but I work hard: I deserve this once in a while." Fair enough, but I prefer places that think more along the lines of providing three squares a day and a dry bed so you can fish. I'm happy with a clapboard lodge where you eat a plain breakfast on a plank table at first light and sleep in a comfortable shack. For one thing, those places are usually cheaper. For another, they leave me feeling less like I've checked into a good hotel and more like I'm out in the sticks having an adventure, which is sort of the whole idea.

Any fishing lodge can be good, but you naturally develop preferences over time. Given the choice, I'll take a smaller lodge over a bigger one. That is, a place that has eight or ten fishermen in for a week instead of an outfit that has thirty or forty. This has less to do with the fishing than you might think. High-volume lodges usually have access to enough water and fish for everyone. It's just that a crowd that size in a remote location can be oppressive and at mealtimes the dining room can resemble a factory cafeteria.

I prefer older lodges to newer ones. For one thing, they often have the weathered, lived in, just barely out of the elements feel I like with lemmings living under the front steps and bats in the rafters. For another, places that have survived for a while probably know what they're doing and have sent home lots of happy fishermen to tell their friends. And if the place doesn't exactly run like a finely tuned sports car, it at least runs like an old pickup that's owned by a good shade-tree mechanic.

It's not a requirement, but I prefer a place with a dog or two. Camp dogs are usually happy and friendly, and a kind word, a pat and maybe a few table scraps will give you a loyal pal for the duration. The only exception to that rule so far was a husky/wolf hybrid on the Agulawok River in Alaska that just plain scared me.

I usually end up at fly-fishing lodges because that's how I fish, but over the years I've had some excellent trips to places that don't cater to fly fishers. This goes more smoothly now than it once did. Over the last thirty or forty years, the sport has become ubiquitous, so even gear guides have some idea of what to do with a fly caster and, unlike in the 1970s, burly sports are less likely to say mean things about "those hippies with their sissy rods." I also think game fish that have grown suspicious of lures and spoons over the last few decades are still pushovers for fur and feathers. Or at least that's how it seems.

Speaking of the seventies, I can remember when communication at remote lodges consisted of a staticky shortwave radio that wouldn't work on rainy days or when the northern lights were especially bright. That was always fine with me. One of the things I like about fishing lodges is the headspace that comes from being profoundly out of touch. Many places now have satellite phones that are more reliable, but I know a lodge owner who tells his clients that the sat phone is reserved for emergencies only, not for checking to see how the kids' soccer games turned out or for calling their brokers. He once said to me, "If these people can't be away from a phone for a week, they shouldn't have come, right?"

But emergencies do happen, regardless of how careful everyone is. I once fished at a lodge where, a few years earlier, a plane had crashed in a sudden storm, killing the pilot and several passengers. I won't say everyone was still depressed, but when your worst fear comes true, it does permanently change the atmosphere. At a lodge in Canada the floatplane I'd flown in the year before blew a piston on takeoff and went down in the trees across the lake. It was a freak accident—the plane had just recently been serviced, inspected and certified airworthy. Everyone on board was hurt, but no one was killed. And at another place a man got seriously ill and couldn't be flown out to a hospital right away because the floatplane was grounded by weather. They did finally get him out, but too late.

No one was at fault. Those were just examples of what can happen. This possibility of real trouble explains any number of things: why some lodge managers simply smile at complaints about scratchy towels and underdone pasta, why you may be asked to sign a liability waiver when you go to a lodge and why many lodges now have the best communication available. But of course technology can, and inevitably does, go too far.

I was at a lodge in Alaska recently that was close enough to a small, year-round settlement to have satellite TV and cellphone reception as well as wireless internet service. This may turn out to be the wave of the future, but I'd never seen anything like it before. We all caught fish, but in the evenings, instead of talking about them in front of the fireplace, everyone was busy texting, calling, e-mailing, watching TV or playing video games while I played the solitary Luddite, finding a quiet place to read or sitting on the porch waiting for a bear to shamble out of the darkening forest.

I've met people at lodges who became close friends, I've gotten along with people I wouldn't have liked if we hadn't been thrown together by chance and of course I've run across a few stupendous assholes. I've spent evenings arguing, laughing, reminiscing and now and then sulking over a run of bad luck. I've endured unsuccessful attempts at entertainment. (Karaoke Night above the Arctic Circle is still a painful memory.) I've also formed temporary partnerships and alliances and now and then banded together with others to ostracize an especially nasty drunk or blowhard in a north woods version of *Lord of the Flies*. But I've never before been to a lodge that reminded me of a hotel lobby full of strangers.

12

TEMPORARY PURIST

I live near the confluence of two perfectly good freestone trout creeks in the Rocky Mountains, but in early April when the midges are still on and the first of the blue-winged olive mayflies could be starting, the grass seems greener on the small tailwater in the next drainage north. This isn't a long drive as drives to rivers go, but it involves going twenty-some miles up my own canyon—gaining over 2,000 feet in elevation in the process—crossing the saddle above

Muggins Gulch, then looping around Mount Olympus and down into the next draw.

In the kind of chilly, low-ceilinged spring weather that's thought to be best for hatches, this trip also involves driving the narrow canyon road up into the sensory deprivation of the cloud cover. I know the route by heart, but when visibility is down to thirty feet, landmarks dissolve, one bend in the road looks a lot like another and I can catch myself wondering, is this Split Rock, or am I already at Lion Gulch?

I'm not a fast mountain driver even in the best conditions, but I'm really creeping along now; peering ahead into the fog for a glimmer of taillights going even slower than I am, for the deer, elk and occasional bighorn sheep that are all possible obstructions on this road, not to mention the odd bike rider pumping uphill with his Spandex-clad ass aimed lewdly at my windshield.

I also know that this wet spring weather lubricates canyon walls, causing them to shed a winter's worth of frost-heaved rocks. These can be anything from a scattering of sharp granite pebbles in your lane to a car-sized boulder to a road-blocking landslide, none of which you want to come upon too suddenly. If you have any romance at all in your soul, the mountains in fog are hauntingly beautiful, but it's best to keep your eyes on the road instead of mooning over the landscape.

So it takes longer to get there than usual, but now that I'm down off the back side of the saddle, the visibility has improved a little. When I cross the bridge a few hundred yards below Olympus Dam, I can see that the river is flowing clear and right around a hundred cubic feet per second, even though the dam itself is just a faint shape in the mist. This is a perfect flow. It's low enough for the trout to rise freely if they have a reason to, but still high enough to keep them from being any spookier or leader-shy than they already are.

The last time I was here, the midge hatch was still going strong. I fished dry flies all afternoon and landed maybe half a dozen brown and rainbow trout, two of which were good-sized for this river. The first of the blue-winged olives were also just starting to sputter off to the tune of one mayfly every few minutes. It wasn't even what you'd call a sparse hatch, but the bugs were an inkling of things to come.

It's now a week later and a textbook dry-fly day: thickly overcast, chilly and windless with the falling barometer fishermen believe makes trout bite. When I pull off to have a closer look at the river, it doesn't seem to be drizzling at all, but after standing there for a few minutes I wipe the shoulder of my jacket and my hand comes away wet. The same thing will happen to an insect's wings. Olives and midges like to hatch in weather like this, even though their wings dry more slowly than they would in more typically bright Colorado weather, leaving them on the water longer, where the trout can get them. It's just before noon on a day when you'd expect an afternoon hatch. The canyon looks like a Sung Dynasty Chinese watercolor, and the river seems to be humming with anticipation—or maybe it's just me.

Four hours later I haven't seen a single fly or so much as one rising trout—not even a dink in a foamy backwater. I'm not so much disappointed as I am puzzled and a little embarrassed. Everything I think I know about the local trout fishing tells me that hundreds of fish should be rising to a multiple hatch and they're not. All the usual signs are aligned, including the skanky spring weather at 8,000 feet. Since I left home, it's gone from fog to mist to drizzle to a light, steady rain. In the next few hours the precipitation will go the full distance from rain to sleet to the granular pellets known as graupel to outright snow after dark. To people from other parts of the country, the phrase "springtime in the Rockies" accurately conjures mountain meadows full of wildflowers, but not the fifty-seven inches of April snow that watered them.

Of course we never know what to expect when we go fishing and wouldn't *want* to know if we could. We spend enormous amounts of energy trying to predict the future for fun and profit, but if we really knew with any certainty how our careers, love lives, the stock market or the fishing would turn out, we'd die of boredom. The best thing about fishing is that it takes place entirely in the present tense, so even if you feel vaguely cheated, you're not brooding about the past, worrying about the future or wondering, What am I doing here? A question that's only asked by those who wish they were somewhere else.

After checking here and there along the upper river with no luck, I end up staking out one of the best dry-fly runs in the canyon, still without seeing a rise. I'm standing knee-deep in the water by way of claiming the spot, but that's not really necessary. There were some other fishermen around earlier, but most bailed by midafternoon when the hatch failed to materialize. For the last few hours, I've been stubbornly rigged with a size 20 parachute mayfly pattern and a size 22 midge emerger on a dropper to split the difference, but I've yet to make a cast.

The canyon is eerily quiet. The chilly air is still, rain is falling silently and fog muffles the sound of the current. Several Audubon's warblers that weren't here last week are perched on river birch twigs overlooking the water. These little insect-eating birds have recently made the long, harrowing flight from Central America to northern Colorado. They didn't all survive the trip, and those that did are now bone-tired and starving and are also waiting for a hatch. I, on the other hand, am well rested, well fed and have nothing important at stake. I'm simply here in my capacity as the hapless goofball, considering the casual brutality of nature while rainwater drips off the brim of my hat.

It does occur to me that I might still catch a few fish if I were willing to pinch on weight and dredge with nymphs, which for once I'm not. I understand that to fit the profile of the modern fly fisherman I should be less the long-suffering sportsman-philosopher and more the conspicuous fanatic carpet-bombing the river with the latest fly patterns, tackle and techniques: fishing from the same impulse that makes professional baseball players take steroids.

I'll admit that I'm capable of that from time to time, even though many of my fly patterns are dated and my tackle isn't the newest or the best money can buy, although in some cases it's the best money could have bought in 1968. I'll also say that with forty years of experience I do know how to fish with a fly rod and I'm actually not a bad nymph fisherman. It's just that some of the first dependable dry-fly fishing of the year begins in April and after a winter of bouncing split shot on the bottoms of rivers, I'm ready enough for a change to become a seasonal purist.

This kind of temporary piety is the best I can muster these days, but I wasn't always like that. Way back when, I took one of my first halting steps from bait to flies on a small, fast-flowing mountain stream where the trout were small, numerous and none too smart. I had only the sketchiest idea of what I was doing, but I actually caught one on something like a size 14 Adams. At the time, I didn't understand how forgiving those fish were, so I was deeply impressed with myself. On the strength of a single eight-inch brook trout, I eschewed all lesser forms of fishing and immediately became a born again dry-fly fisherman.

I like to think it came down to prettiness. I'd taken up fly fishing in the first place because in the right hands it was just about the loveliest thing I'd ever seen. The same went for dry flies. They looked like angels with their perky wings and hackle and they exhibited the ingenious engineering that allowed you to actually float a steel hook on the surface of the water.

I also liked the relative unlikelihood of hooking a trout on a dry fly. At the time, some fishing expert had written that trout do 80 percent of their feeding under water and only 20 percent on the surface. That was probably just an educated guess, but the numbers stuck and made dry-fly fishing look like one $80 bottle of wine compared to four cases of Thunderbird for the same price. (It also made nymph fishing seem like more of a sure thing than it really is, but I wouldn't learn that until later.) Something similar had happened a few years earlier when it was said that only 1 percent of motorcyclists gave the rest a bad name and the outlaw bikers immediately began displaying "1%" patches on their greasy denim jackets.

There was an irresistible air of artistry to dry-fly fishing, although I now think it's more of a neat trick than an actual art form. If a good fly fisherman was the picture of efficiency, a dry-fly fisherman was someone who had put efficiency in its proper place without actually turning his back on it. He could, and would, wait out a rise of trout using the superior patience it takes to successfully delay gratification. He might eventually get cagey enough to know when and where the hatches would come off and arrive at the river half an hour before the first dimple appeared on the surface. On the right water at the right time of year, he might even manage to pound fish up to a dry fly even when they weren't already rising on their own, which still strikes me as the ultimate con.

The idea wasn't to go to a river and make something happen; it was to be there when it happened of its own accord and then slip in almost unnoticed. You could chase a hatch for days or even weeks, and then when it finally came off, you'd stand there and let one fish start rising, then three or four, then ten or twelve. You wanted them to lull themselves into a comfortable rhythm so they'd be less suspicious when you finally started casting, and sometimes it was only when a hatch got going that the bigger fish would show themselves. Out of curiosity (and because you had time to kill) you'd learn about birds and wildflowers. You'd tell yourself that even a blank day on the water could be a beautiful thing, and sometimes it was.

Dry-fly fishing took the kind of composure that was a stretch at the age I was then. By all rights, patience should come easily when you're young because you have all the time in the world, but in practice it only arrives later when time begins to stretch a little thin. Still, the effort seemed worthwhile as a kind of counterculture self-improvement project, and my friends and I were only vaguely aware that we were updating a tradition. To the previous generation, the whole dry-fly business had been genteel and vaguely British in the spirit of Izaak Walton. We operated on more of an oriental model along the lines of Sun Tzu, the ancient Chinese strategist who's supposed to have said, "If you sit on the riverbank long enough, the body of your enemy will float by."

Of course, few of us have what it takes to wait indefinitely for the body of our enemy—whoever or whatever we think that is—to float by, but if you're waiting out a hatch, you can still say you're "doing something" in the hyperactive way Americans use that term. Coincidentally, that's also the legal definition. Even if you're not casting and don't even have a fly tied on, if a wildlife officer catches you anywhere near public water with a rod in your hand, he'll assume you're fishing and you had damned well better have a fishing license.

Being young, eager and impressionable must have had something to do with it, too. I became a dry-fly fisher—and also decided to make my way in life as a writer—at an age when you can easily make life-altering choices that might later seem suicidally impractical. Fly fishing seemed terribly important then (and still does), but it was just part of a larger program of relearning some of the rustic skills the last generation of my family had intentionally *un*learned in the suburbs. I thought that finding something better than the usual uneasy truce with life and livelihood was my own unique idea, only to learn that I was part of a loose movement of disaffected young folks who'd all had the same brainstorm. Naturally, there were misgivings. For one thing, I was poor as dirt, with no real prospects, but if one day I was afraid the world would pass me by, the next day I was afraid it *wouldn't*.

Some choices never actually prove to be right or wrong, but they do become irrevocable, and even if you don't believe in fate, things eventually seem to turn out the way they were meant to. In the end, the world visited briefly enough to put a roof over my head and passed by to the extent that I feel I've retained my sanity. I may not always be deliriously happy, but I'm content enough that I've never had to "seek professional help," as they say. That's just as well. After talking to any number of friends who *have* seen psychiatrists, it seems clear that you can't start with a middle-aged basket case and reverse-engineer a different life.

But eventually that initial flush of purism that afflicts all beginners ran its course—as it probably should have—and I came to see that no one fishing method is superior to any other. Nymphs, streamers, mice, wet flies and everything in between were all effective at times and all had their own apparently infinite shades of subtlety. Even short-lining live maggots on a cane pole, as some locals did then, incorporated all the skills of trout fishing as well as a particular sensitivity to the strike.

I once heard a dry-fly fisherman say, "You can catch 'em ugly or you can catch 'em pretty." I agree, but I now think that catching 'em pretty has more to do with a kind of seamless elegance than with what's tied to the end of your leader. How you decide to fly-fish on any given day is one of those rare things that needn't concern anyone else. It's yours alone and the only rule is that if there's something you love, you should do as much of it as you can—the same rationale that works so well for Labrador retrievers.

So I now consider myself a generalist, but I still have a soft spot for dry flies simply because that's how all this started. Likewise, I was with a dark-haired girl on that first memorable night in the back row at the drive-in, so brunettes will rattle my cage for the rest of my natural life. This is less than a pathological fixation, but somehow more than just a preference. There's nothing I can do about it and nothing I *should* do.

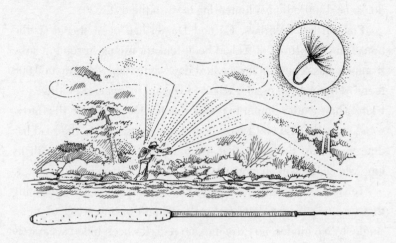

13

TENKARA

We were in my kitchen in northern Colorado on a warm August evening. I was at the stove stirring a pot of elk spaghetti sauce; Susan McCann, the journalist and editor I've lived with for the last twenty years, was constructing an enormous salad; and Ed Engle, the fishing writer and my oldest continuous friend, was slicing French bread. Daniel Galhardo, owner and founder of Tenkara USA, had offered to help several times, but it was a small, crowded kitchen with cats underfoot and limited counter space, and there was nothing left to do, so he'd settled for volunteering to wash the dishes.

For the last few days, Ed and Daniel had been staying at the house, and the three of us had been tenkara fishing in some nearby trout streams. The plan for the next day was to four-wheel up to 9,000 feet to a brook trout creek Ed and I like, and to that end I'd drive to a friend's house after dinner to borrow his Jeep Wrangler. In the thirty-some years that Ed and I have been fishing this stream, the road has deteriorated to the point that my four-wheel-drive pickup with its long wheelbase will no longer make it without bottoming out.

Tenkara is a traditional Japanese method of fixed-line fly fishing that uses only a long, light rod with a length of line attached and a single fly. No guides, no extra line, no reel. It's been billed accurately as the soul of simplicity: the fly-fishing equivalent of haiku. This method—or something very much like it—has been practiced in the mountain streams of Japan for at least several hundred years and may date back as far as the eighth or ninth century.

The original rods were unsplit bamboo and the lines were braided horsehair. They were similar to the rods described in *The Treatise of Fishing with an Angle* in 1496 and by any number of other cultures around the world that used artificial flies, although the advantage Japan had over Europe was that they could use bamboo instead of hardwood, so from the beginning the rods were lighter and more delicate. It's conceivable that there was some cross-pollination between cultures that would explain the similarity in tackle, but it seems more likely that when first confronted with the question of how to deliver a feathered hook to a fish using available technology, the universal answer has always been: Get a long stick and a string.

Tenkara wouldn't have been considered a sport at first. It's said to have been developed by people who simply wanted fish to eat or sell, so there was no need for the embellishments you find in things that are done more for fun than results. The rod itself could be found growing wild, and collected rather than bought. There was no need for more than a rod's length of line because the mountain streams these anglers fished, and the trout and char they caught, were both fairly small. A tenkara rod was a tool: as utilitarian as a hoe or a shovel and no more complicated than it had to be. Even the apparently ornamental wraps may have been originally intended to camouflage the outline of the rod rather than to look pretty.

The modern incarnation of tenkara *is* considered a sport, but although it's gone somewhat high-tech, it hasn't lost its homespun simplicity. The rods are now telescoping graphite, usually between eleven and fourteen feet long, inspired by some of the traditional bamboo versions where smaller sections were stored inside larger ones to make the rods more portable. The lines are either braided fluorocarbon—like a long furled leader—or sometimes just level lengths of fluorocarbon that have a smaller diameter and are said to cast better in the wind. But high-tech or not, a Japanese angler from three hundred years ago would recognize the tackle.

Daniel said he learned to fly-fish with a conventional fly rod and reel in his native Brazil as a teenager. Later, while living in San Francisco, he got interested in Japanese styles of fly fishing and first learned about tenkara from an old pamphlet published by the English Board of Tourism in 1939. When he traveled to Japan with his wife, Margaret Kuwata, in 2008, he saw tenkara firsthand and was smitten by its elegant simplicity. He doesn't describe this as a conversion experience, but he now fishes exclusively with tenkara tackle, although he's held onto his old rod and reel for sentimental reasons.

Daniel founded Tenkara USA in 2009, marketing the few things a tenkara fisherman needs: rod, line, a handful of flies and not much else. (Tenkara is a traditional Japanese method, but oddly—though maybe not surprisingly—the rods are made in China.) It was also in that year that Daniel met the renowned tenkara fisherman Dr. Hisao Ishigaki when the Doctor spoke at the Catskill Fly Fishing Center in

New York. Daniel and Ishigaki hit it off as student and teacher and now jokingly refer to each other as *"tenkara no otto-san"* and *"tenkara no musuko"* or "tenkara father" and "tenkara son."

Ishigaki is sometimes referred to as a "tenkara master," but that's an unofficial title. In fact, he makes no special claims for himself or for tenkara beyond the method's austere efficiency. Some Americans can't help but imbue the sport with oriental ideology, but when Daniel asked him if there was a Zen aspect to tenkara, Ishigaki laughed and said, "No Zen, just a nice way to catch fish"—which of course is exactly what a Zen master would say.

Daniel himself is young, lean, fit, and seems shy at first, but then turns out to be only soft-spoken. He comes off as a kind of low-key evangelist and his enthusiasm can be quietly infectious, but he's not unaware of the difficulties of introducing something small, quiet and simple to a country that likes things big, loud and complicated. He also understands the dangers inherent in turning something you love into a business, but doesn't seem worried about it. So far, he hasn't launched the big media blitz, which I suspect is equal parts economics and temperament, but he has the obligatory website and blog, he's run a few ads, has done a few interviews and sometimes turns up at fly-fishing trade shows.

Tenkara isn't widely known in America, but word-of-mouth is spreading and in certain circles it has a kind of underground buzz. Over the last year or so, I've run into a number of fly fishers who have heard of tenkara and a smaller handful who've tried it. Attitudes range from shrugging indifference through various levels of curiosity to a newfound dedication to simplicity, though this isn't widespread enough to have flooded the market with used rods and reels. Most said they learned about it on the Internet, and when I searched "tenkara" recently out of curiosity, I got just short of forty thousand results.

There's also been some resistance. A famous fisherman said tenkara was a fad that would blow itself out in a few seasons—a hard case to make about something that's been established practice for centuries. Others have flatly declared that it's not really fly fishing without specifying exactly why.

Converts, on the other hand, brag about the ease of the method and the number of fish they catch. Another well-known fisherman recently said, "I can teach your granddaughter to fish with a tenkara in two minutes and she'll catch more than you."

A collapsed tenkara rod is only about twenty inches long—a stubby graphite shaft with a cork grip that resembles the butt section of a multipiece graphite rod with the reel seat sawn off. When you first extend one, it keeps coming and coming until it begins to feel unwieldy. The line is attached by girth-looping the butt end to a short piece of knotted cord called a "lillian" that sticks straight out of the end of the tip section. The leader is attached to the line with a loop-to-loop connection. You can use whatever length leader you want, but it's best to start with a tippet that doesn't extend much more than a foot or two past the butt of the rod. It's all pretty self-evident, but it doesn't hurt to read the instructions.

The cast is a familiar fly cast, but with a shorter, softer stroke and a high, reaching stop designed to keep the line and most of the leader off the water. It's easy to overpower the rod, and your inbred tendency to shoot an extra foot or two, even on a short forward cast, is stymied by the fixed line. At the end of every cast, your left hand reflexively reaches for the loose line off the reel that isn't there. This may get annoying enough that you'll put your line hand in your pocket to make it stop.

The first time I fished a tenkara rod was in March, during a midge hatch on a small local tailwater. The long, whippy rod and fixed line seemed awkward at first, but I got used to them quickly. The usual repertoire of overhead, sidearm, tuck and pile casts all worked, as well as that flipping aerial roll cast small-stream fishers use and that no one I know has a name for. This was actually the same way I fish pocket water with the usual seven-foot nine-inch or eight-foot rod: making short casts and high-stick drifts with little more than a rod's length of line. The only difference was that with a thirteen-foot rod, a short cast was noticeably longer and I could hold more line off the water for a better, longer drift.

Playing and landing small fish was the kind of thing you'd work out on your own even if you hadn't been told how to do it. You fight the fish against the bend of the rod, and when it's played out, you lift the rod until you can reach the line, hold the line against the rod with one hand and run the other hand down to your trout. Some tenkara fishermen carry a small, round landing net with an offset handle called a *tamo*. Nine times out of ten, it's not necessary, but when it *is* necessary, you're real glad to have it.

It's been said that anyone can learn to fish adequately with a tenkara rod in a few hours, and that may not be an exaggeration. These things are recognizable fly rods, and the more you know about fly fishing in general and tenkara specifically, the more you can get out of them, but they still bear a vague family resemblance to a cane pole and string and are therefore something a seven-year-old could master instinctively. In fact, Daniel said he sells a fair number of rods to hikers and backpackers who aren't exactly dedicated fly fishermen but who like the idea of a complete fishing outfit that packs down small and only weighs a few ounces.

He's also careful to point out that tenkara rods are intended specifically for small water and fish not much more than a foot long, so I wasn't sure that tailwater would be entirely tenkara-friendly. It was a little too wide to be called a small stream and although the average trout is around ten or twelve inches long, you could easily hook a bigger fish. But as it turned out, the water was still low in March, the wading was easy, and with a little more than twenty-six feet of rod and line, there weren't many places I couldn't reach. I also didn't hook a trout longer than ten inches on that first day.

There was another unforeseen advantage. This was a cold, humid day at an elevation of around 8,000 feet, and as we strung up our rods at the car, my friend Vince said, "I hope my line doesn't freeze in the guides." I held up the long rod with no guides and said, "No worries here."

It was only a week or so later on the same river that I did hook a fish I couldn't land. It was a rainbow I'll guess at around seventeen inches and when it made a strong run, I instinctively pointed the rod at him to give him line, remembering too late that I didn't have any more line to give. (Apparently there's no tenkara equivalent to the screaming reel.) Of course, with the rod pointed straight at the fish, he came up tight, neatly snapped off the fly, and kept going. I've lost countless fish over the years and none of them were the end of the world, although they all felt like it at the time. This isn't the old cliché about the big one getting away; it's just that the one that does get away is suddenly the one you really wanted.

Sometime later Ed explained that you should keep your rod up even on a heavy fish, and that this wasn't just a case of horse 'em and hope for the best. Between the flex of the long, light rod, a little stretch in the braided line, and the cushion of your own wrist and elbow, you can actually lay into a bigger trout much harder than you think. Also, a fish can only go in the direction he's pointed, and the reach of the long rod lets you deflect a run and steer the fish into slack water. It does take practice but finally boils down to a little knowledge of fish behavior, a feel for the capabilities of the tackle and the accurate snap judgment. You can still hook a fish you can't land, but once you know how to use the rod, that fish gets considerably larger.

Daniel suggests using only light leaders because it *is* possible to break these long, delicate rods (he markets replacement sections), but of course not everyone follows his advice. He said he's heard from customers who claim to have landed unusually large fish on tenkara rods: twenty-inch trout, small steelhead, some bonefish and a largemouth bass weighing eight pounds. He seemed to have mixed feelings about that, but when his wife landed her own twenty-inch rainbow on a tenkara rod, he was eager to show me the photos.

As it turned out, Ed and I had stumbled on tenkara independently, which was no surprise to me. We've known each other for something like thirty-five years and share, among other things, a long-running interest in traditional Japanese art, poetry and philosophy that dates back to our counterculture days in the 1970s. (This year we coincidentally sent each other the same Christmas card featuring a winter scene by Japanese woodblock artist Kawase Hasui.) It was only natural that with something like this in the air, we'd have both caught the same scent. It was also just like Ed to have worked out some things that I'd missed.

I fished tenkara rods off and on through the season, taking plenty of time off for bigger water and bigger fish where I wanted a longer cast and a reel with backing and a good drag. Switching back and forth became seamless. Like any specialized tackle, a tenkara rod is versatile and efficient in the range of conditions it was intended for, but it becomes less so as you deviate from the ideal until eventually its advantages become frustrations and you feel like breaking the thing over your knee.

I was surprised at how quickly I absorbed the novelty of tenkara and ended up just fishing. Early on, I'd sometimes giggle out loud at the long reach I had and the beautiful drifts I was getting in normally difficult pocket water, but then I just got used to it. Playing and landing most of the trout I hooked was straightforward enough, and now and then I'd get one that provided the kind of drama that keeps you fishing. I'm not sure I caught any more fish than usual with the tenkara rod, but on the right kind of water I was more likely to do it with that elusive smoothness we all strive for.

By the time Daniel came out to fish in August, I thought I'd become a reasonably adept tenkara fisherman. I'd learned to cast in fairly tight quarters, to keep my fly out of the trees (usually) and to play and land fish deftly. I'd also picked up the neat trick of collapsing the rod and coiling the line around my hand to bushwhack through thick bankside brush, which alone is worth the price of admission. I'd lost a few fish, but I couldn't blame any of them on the tackle. I'd also landed trout up to fifteen inches in fast current and had watched Ed bring in a sixteen-inch splake. It turned out that hooking a fish on a tenkara rod was a surprisingly businesslike procedure. You'd either land the fish or lose it, but either way it would happen quickly.

I'd even prepared a succinct explanation about this strange rod I was using for fishermen who were curious, but oddly, no one ever asked.

I'd been fishing the usual sparse selection of flies in my small-stream box on an upstream or across-stream dead drift—usually a single dry fly, sometimes with a nymph dropper. I'd also done well a few times fishing a wet fly on a short down and across-current swing and dredging shallow pockets with a brace of nymphs. In other words, I was fishing the way I always fished, only with slightly different tackle.

Daniel said he also started out with his old favorite patterns, but after a second trip to Japan, he switched to tenkara flies. These are the simplest imaginable patterns, often just a thread or floss body with a reversed hackle that flares forward over the eye of the hook. A few of these patterns have a flash of color, but most are drab and plain as dirt. What Daniel calls a "pure tenkara fisherman" is a total presentationist and may do all his fishing with a single one of these patterns, carrying two or three identical spares of the same size in a small glass vial with a cork stopper and fishing them dry or wet as needed.

Tenkara flies are traditionally fished on a more or less tight line with a series of subtle swings, skitters and gently pulsing lifts and drops, always keeping in mind that whatever slight motion you make with your rod hand is multiplied by as much as fourteen feet of rod. (It sounds and even looks easy, but the easy part is to overdo it.) In the water the fly looks very much like an insect struggling weakly toward the surface, while the flaring of the reversed soft hackle does a good impression of a breaststroke. The overall effect is convincingly lifelike, and one afternoon I watched Daniel tease up any number of trout on the kind of catch-and-release tailwater where anything but a dead drift is considered to be heresy.

The long rod gives you lots of reach, but there are still times when you need to employ some stealth. There can be lots of crouching and kneeling, and Daniel favors a brand of wader that comes with built-in kneepads. For all its simplicity, the traditional tenkara strategy has an air of impatience. Rather than compulsively changing patterns looking for the right one, you give each fish a shot at biting your one fly, and if it doesn't, you shrug and move on with a distinctly non-American acceptance of the fact that you can't catch them all.

I never did become a pure tenkara fisherman because it didn't seem necessary. There are days when I enjoy the refreshing lack of clutter the method provides, but then there are other days when I find great comfort in the old familiar clutter that has taken me a lifetime to accumulate. In the end, I've come to think of tenkara less as a style of fly fishing and more as a useful thought experiment in which you ask not, How much do I need? but, How little can I get away with?

And along those same lines, there's the obvious paradox that in the ongoing search for a kind of blissful simplicity, I've gone ahead and gotten myself yet another fly rod.

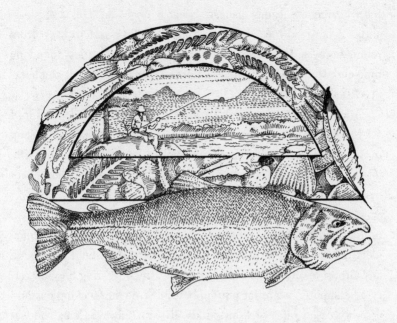

14

KODIAK

Every location on earth has its unique morning sounds. Just before dawn on Uyak Bay on the west coast of Kodiak Island, it's the steady breathing of the surf, a single muffled splash that could be a salmon or maybe a sea otter, the first few herring gulls beginning to wake up, and faintly, from far off across the bay, something that doesn't really sound like elephants trumpeting, but that's the closest comparison I can come up with.

I go back inside the lodge, pour a second cup of coffee and ask

John Pearce, the camp manager, what it might be. He says, pleasantly, "I have no idea" while making a visible effort to keep from rolling his eyes. John has been in the sport fishing business for a long time and would have said that by now he'd heard it all, but elephants in Alaska? Jeez!

A few minutes later when the owner, Bruce Kososki, comes in, I ask him the same question. With the coffeepot in one hand and a cup in the other, he frowns for a moment, then brightens and says, "Oh, it must be sea lions." Of course, sea lions. I give John a triumphant look, which he ignores, and another day of fishing begins.

At about this time the day before, the predawn sounds included muffled crowd noise, recorded announcements and unidentified electronic beeping at the Anchorage airport. This could have been any airport in any city except that businessmen wearing ties and carrying computers were far outnumbered by rougher-looking customers with cased rifles or fishing rods. It wasn't always clear who was coming and who was going except for two men, each with a week's growth of stubble, who were checking enormous moose antlers at the oversized baggage-counter.

I'd flown in from Denver and was on my way to catch the Era Aviation flight out to the town of Kodiak on Kodiak Island. Once we were in the air, the man across the aisle from me got out an expensive-looking, disk-drag fly reel and proceeded to tie on a fresh leader. He looked over and gave me a maniacal grin, which I answered with a thumbs-up. We were two strangers going fishing, and although our respective trips could still go either way, just being in Alaska meant we had upped the ante.

In Kodiak, I walked across the wet parking lot to Island Air Service for the hop across the island to Larsen Bay with its dirt airstrip, Russian Orthodox church complete with an onion-shaped steeple, and thirty-nine year-round residents. Then there was a van ride to the lodge, where I changed into waders, took another short van ride down to the harbor and climbed aboard a lovely 1957 de Havilland Beaver floatplane. We were headed to the source of the Dog Salmon River at Frazer Lake, where I would finally get down to business.

At the lake we strung up 6-weight rods and hiked downstream, talking loudly to let any bears that were around know we were coming. Bears don't like surprises. Nine times out of ten they'll just run away when they're startled, but it's that tenth time you're hoping to avoid. For emergencies, the two fly-fishing guides, Chuck Mercer and Trent Deeter, were each armed with 12-gauge pump shotguns loaded with rifled slugs. Our pilot, Jay Wattum, was carrying a lever-action .45-70 carbine done up for the wet climate in stainless steel with fiberglass stocks. (A tourist brochure on safety in Kodiak bear country warns that the usual .44-magnum hog leg "may not be adequate.") These riot guns were comforting in a way, but you understand that they're a last resort that you'll go to great lengths not to depend on. We Americans can feel naïvely safe when we're packing firearms, but honestly, few of us have either the skill or the nerve to calmly take down a charging bear at a range of twenty-five yards.

We were there for the rainbows and Dolly Vardens that were following the spawning sockeye salmon to feed on their dribbled and dislodged eggs. By then the sockeye run was nearing its end, but that hardly mattered. The rainbows and Dollys had been gorging on eggs from one salmon run or another for most of the summer and were hard-wired to pick up anything small, orange and egglike drifting in the current. That would include our plastic beads rigged slightly ahead of size 10 barbless hooks and slightly behind a single small split shot. There are those who wouldn't consider this a proper fly and in another context I might agree, but Alaskan fly fishers tend to bypass fine points of style in favor of practicality, and the attitude is contagious.

This wasn't the main event for anyone. I'd come in mid-September hoping for silver salmon, the one species of Pacific salmon I'd never caught. Dick Matzke and his two sons, who were also staying at the lodge, had come to winch halibut out of three hundred feet of salt water and shoot Sitka blacktail deer. This side trip was just the kind of harmless showmanship some lodges like to engage in on the first day. By the time most of us have finally gotten where we wanted to be in Alaska, we've spent an inordinate amount of time schlepping from one airplane to the next without a decent meal or much more than a cat-nap. Enthusiasm can still trump exhaustion, but at this point it's a toss-up and catching a whole bunch of beautiful fish without much effort is the surest way to tip the collective mood into positive territory.

After lunch we hiked back to the plane for the short flight down to the mouth of the river to look for silver salmon. (Rivers that rise on islands aren't long because they don't have room to be. No place on Kodiak is more than fifteen miles from the sea.) After we'd banked downriver and over the tidal flat where the Dog entered a small bay, Jay asked over the intercom, "Did you see all the silvers in those first two pools?"

"No," I replied, "I was watching the bear."

"Yeah, the bear's a good sign," he said. "He's lookin' for salmon just like we are."

By the time I'd spotted this big adult, he was already trotting away from the racket of the plane. His brown fur rippled like silk in the thin sunlight, and as he glanced at us over his shoulder, he looked more annoyed than scared.

Jay beached the plane at the edge of an alluvial fan several hun-dred yards from shore, checked the tide chart and announced that we had to be back by four-twenty. Otherwise the outgoing tide would strand us there until tomorrow.

"Can you remember that?" he asked.

"Yeah," I said, "but I don't have a watch."

"That's cool," he said. "Somebody'll have one."

In the days to come, I'd learn that "That's cool" was Jay's auto-matic response to just about everything. Like some other bush pilots

I'd met, Jay could seem like a wing nut on the ground—all bluster and bad jokes—but it was either an act for the benefit of tourists or some kind of Jekyll and Hyde thing because in the air he was all business and there was no one you'd rather have at the controls.

We waded ashore and Chuck checked me out at the top of the second long pool. He said most of the fish would be lying in the deeper current near the far bank about a fifty-foot cast away. He pointed and on cue a large salmon rolled. "Cast down and across, give the fly a minute to sink and strip it back in short jerks," he said.

On my third cast the fly stopped as if it had been slammed in a door and the fish ran downstream and then back up with startling speed, making porpoising jumps and rapping my knuckles with the reel handle. There was the usual moment of panic. The fish seemed too big. The 8-weight rod seemed too small. A few minutes later I had my first silver salmon on the beach: a twelve-pound buck, thick and deep with a grotesquely undershot kype that was the very face of grim determination. He was still within sight of salt water, but already his silver flanks were beginning to flush pink. I'd come on this trip hoping to see a Kodiak bear and catch a silver salmon, and both had happened in the space of twenty minutes. It seemed almost too easy.

The next fish was a chrome-bright female of about ten pounds that had a more troutlike face and fought no less ferociously for being two pounds lighter. There were some others after that and then everyone was reeling in and wading back out toward the plane. I had no idea what time it was, but there was no outgoing current on the flat, so we'd beaten the tide and wouldn't have to spend the night. I glanced over my shoulder for the charging bear my imagination had been concocting all afternoon, but there was nothing but beach grass and driftwood.

One rainy morning we flew out to the Karluk River, skirting a high rock cliff shrouded in mist and then turning south along the Shelikof Strait. We landed on a wide tidal lagoon on the lower river amid no less than a thousand herring gulls, every last one of them alternately picking at a salmon carcass and screaming at the top of its lungs. The riverbank was littered with dead salmon: mostly spawned-out sockeyes—some nearly whole, others just gull-picked skeletons—as well as what was left of some larger silvers that had been recently eaten by bears. The river itself was a thin stew of decomposing fish parts, bear and bird crap and shed gull feathers. It smelled, not unpleasantly, like an alley behind a sushi restaurant.

When I started fishing there were five bears in sight on the far bank: two larger males spread out upstream and a big sow with twin cubs downstream. While we were there, two younger males moseyed around the bend downstream, gave us long, disgusted looks as Trent and Chuck walked toward them yelling "Hey bear! Hey bear!" and then waded casually across the river to the far side, never once glancing back.

Casting along fifty yards of river, I landed several nice-sized sockeyes of five or six pounds. These weren't the fish I was after, but they're so bizarre-looking that they're always fun to catch. When a sockeye enters freshwater and begins to mature sexually, its jaws lengthen and enlarge, its teeth grow big and snarly and its now-deformed head turns a sickly green color. Meanwhile, the body swells up into a tall hump and turns bright red. Compared to the silvery, streamlined ocean form of this fish, a spawning sockeye looks like a werewolf in a Santa Claus suit and is always worth a photo to show the folks back home.

The silvers were lying deeper than the sockeyes in the slow current, and it was possible to target them after a fashion by giving the weighted streamer a little more time to sink. These were bright fish fresh from the salt that would make two or three long, fast, angry runs before they tired enough for the bulldogging endgame.

At first I thought it was just my imagination when, after a couple of hours, the current seemed to slow down. By the time it stopped altogether and then began flowing in the opposite direction, I'd figured out on my own that the tide was coming in. The fishing shut off abruptly, and as I continued to cast without a strike, a particularly gruesome dead sockeye that had drifted past fifteen minutes earlier bobbed by going the other way.

On the flight back we made a detour to scout for more silvers. We flew up the Zachar River with our right wingtip tight to one ridge. That happens a lot and it used to make me nervous until I learned the reason for it. From time to time a pilot flying up a narrow valley is faced with the necessity of turning around because of weather, engine trouble or whatever. If he's out in the middle of the valley, he may not have room to bank in either direction without hitting one ridge or the other, but if he's hugging one side, there's a better chance he'll have room to turn.

We didn't spot any salmon, so we banked over a low saddle and flew down another smaller stream toward Brown's Lagoon. It was just a boggy trickle at first, but it took on more volume until, a half mile from the mouth, it widened into a single long bend pool with a dark stripe down the outside that Chuck said was a pod of maybe a hundred silvers.

Back at the lodge the crew was busy cleaning halibut, the largest of which weighed about eighty pounds, and on the porch outside the mudroom I nearly tripped over the caped-out head of a nice blacktail buck. It had been a good day all around.

That evening a friend of the owner's, a commercial fisherman named Pete, came to dinner. He was just what you'd expect: ropy arms, big chest, frost-colored beard on a wind-burned face and dressed only in a T-shirt on a chilly, rainy evening. When we were introduced, we looked at each other suspiciously, and Pete asked, "Do we know each other?" I said I thought maybe we did, but I couldn't quite place him either.

We eyeballed each other all through the meal and afterward went out on the porch in a light drizzle to pick this thing apart. It took an hour of comparing lifetimes, but we decided we could only have known each other in passing in San Francisco in the summer of 1964, which would also account for our fuzzy memories. Maybe we ran into each other at parties or free concerts, or the City Lights Bookstore, or the Coexistence Bagel Shop or even at the very corner of Haight and Ashbury itself. We probably hadn't been close friends, but we'd have had to be more than just faces in the crowd to each other for the memory to have stuck this long. We stared at each other in the light leaking from the warm, dry lodge, wondering what forgotten adventures we might have shared. And here we were forty-six years later in Alaska: gray-haired survivors, alive and well and each chasing salmon in our own way and for our own reasons. It was heavy, man.

The next morning Trent, Chuck and I were dropped off at Brown's Lagoon by a party of saltwater fishermen from the lodge with the promise that they'd pick us up at high tide in the afternoon. We hiked upstream through a narrow canyon that at low tide was steep-sided and slippery with mud and kelp. At the top of this cut, we broke out into a pretty valley ringed with low, forested mountains half hidden in clouds and followed the little river upstream to the pool full of salmon we'd seen from the air the day before.

As we strolled around the last bend, we came face-to-face with a large bear at a range of about thirty yards. I yelled "Bear!" more or less pointlessly and the crack in my voice made it a two-syllable word. The bear, bless his heart, turned around and trotted off upstream.

We walked on to the pool, where I tied on a fly, being careful with my knot while staying peripherally hyperaware of my surroundings. Kodiaks are apex predators and a big adult male like the one we'd just seen can weigh as much as fifteen hundred pounds. They make a strong and lasting impression. I caught two bright silvers on a handful of casts, one from the bottom of the run, the other from the top.

Then we sat on the bank to rest the water. We'd already decided this was the best strategy. There might be the odd salmon somewhere upstream, but aerial recognizance had suggested that this was the one and only honey hole.

This turned out to be a sublime afternoon of fishing. I'd catch two big, hot salmon; then we'd relax on the bank for the better part of an hour to let the pod settle down while talking about the things fishermen talk about. I learned that Chuck and Trent had known each other back home in Montana and that Trent was the older of the two at a venerable thirty-one. Chuck didn't volunteer his age, but Trent said he was as young as his baby face made him look and not a bad-looking kid, really, except for that great big head. Chuck smiled patiently, apparently having endured this baby-faced, bigheaded business all season.

I kept looking around nervously and finally said I was worried that the bear was still back in the trees behind us, stewing about being run out of the only pool on the river that held salmon and maybe even working up a grudge about it. Trent said he'd been thinking the same thing, but that he was more concerned that when he'd talked to his girlfriend by satellite phone last night, she'd used "the M word." That would be marriage, not money.

I ended up landing six big silvers, the largest weighing somewhere in the high teens, and one lonely little pink salmon that had shown up late for the party. All his potential mates and rivals were already spawned out and dead on the bank, their bones picked clean by birds and their skulls leering vacantly at the sky. I felt sort of sorry for him.

On the last pass through the pool, the hot-pink streamer I'd been fishing all week finally stopped working and Chuck suggested I try a different pattern: basically the same lead-eyed rabbit-fur-and-tinsel number, except in purple. I asked him what the two patterns were called. He said he didn't know and, this being Alaska and all, they might not even *have* names. Then he added, "Tell you what, let's call the pink one the Haight and the purple one the Ashbury for old time's sake."

My biggest silver came on the last day, which is a nice way for it to happen. We were back on the Karluk, and I tied into a salmon that ran so far and fast that at first I thought I'd foul-hooked a big sockeye. Trent and Chuck thought the same thing until we saw it was an extremely large male silver with the fly fairly in its jaw, at which point things got serious for a few minutes. When we finally got the fish on the beach, Chuck called it at "Less than twenty pounds, but not too much less" and one of the bigger silvers he'd ever seen.

I don't always have the presence of mind to quit on a good fish, but it was late on the last day and my wrist and forearm ached from playing salmon, so I reeled in and found a rock to sit on. Once in a great while fishing can seem like a possible route to the virtues of clarity and restraint. Or maybe there are just times when enough is enough. In any case, I wanted to let this last one sink in, not as a set of weights and measures or a number on the way to the final score, but as a singular, flesh-and-blood fish with a life of its own.

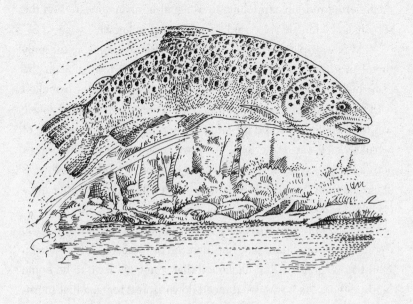

15

MONTANA

We were driving over a dirt-road pass through the Salt River Mountains in Wyoming: two muddy wheelruts running next to the stream we'd fished that afternoon, which, this high up the drainage, was narrow enough to straddle. It was near sunset on a clear September evening, and as we started down the backside of the pass, the valley ahead of us was a bowl of purple shade trimmed in gold. Doug reached over and turned on the GPS unit in the pickup. A meandering red line stretching to a digital horizon appeared on the screen, and a female voice said, "Street name unknown."

It was well past dark by the time we found rooms at the only motel in a three-block-long, partially boarded-up town out on the state highway. Dinner was microwaved frozen pizza at a bar filled with roughnecks and cowhands where the country and western music was loud enough to rattle the windows and the betting on a game of 8-ball seemed way too serious. The town cop was sitting in his cruiser across the street, waiting to break up a fight or pick off drunk drivers at closing time. Meanwhile, he was relaxing with a cup of coffee and a cigar, enjoying the peace and quiet while it lasted.

If I'd had my way, we'd have been camped on that last stream so we could fish one more day, but then the drawback to a four-person road trip is the increased likelihood that some will have to be home before others. As it was, we'd raced down from Montana that morning and spent a few hours on a lovely piece of cutthroat trout water that deserved at least two full days. The plan was to put on another fifty or sixty miles yet that evening, find a place to stay the night and then make it home to northern Colorado with a few hours to spare. It was the kind of rush job that makes you wonder if the quickie can play any positive role in a contemplative sport.

As it turned out, everyone landed a few pretty Snake River cutthroats and we were back on the road only an hour and a half later than we'd planned. I was the one who held things up. By the time I got back, everyone was already out of their waders with their gear packed and milling around the pickup impatiently. I said I'd lost track of the time, which they understood to mean that I hadn't really lost track of the time but knew they wouldn't leave without me.

This had been a high runoff year in the West and we weren't the only fishermen who were running around late in the season trying to be everywhere at once before winter locked it all up again. In my home drainage on Colorado's northern East Slope, the spring snowpack was measured at 343 percent of normal—the highest ever recorded. In other parts of the Rockies it was more like 250 percent; maybe not biblical proportions, but enough to extend the runoff far into what should have been dry-fly season. Even in mid-August, trout that would normally be sipping mayflies were acting more like catfish: holding deep in brown water and feeding by scent and feel. In many streams, fishing anything short of a gob of worms and a sinker had begun to seem like an exercise in style.

Runoff is normally a good time to travel to other parts of the West, but this year the entire continental mountain range was more or less in the same boat. An August trip to Idaho was canceled outright when the guide said he had no idea when, or even if, the river would come into shape. A July trip to Montana was tentatively postponed until September because, as our contact said, "There are only two rivers in the state that are fishable and everyone in Montana with a fly rod is already there."

It brings a man low to live in good trout country and not be able to find a place to fish near home. Some tailwaters held out for a while after the freestone streams got high and muddy, but as the reservoirs filled to capacity with runoff, dams were opened to flush the excess water. ("Excess water" is not a term you normally hear in a semiarid climate.) One small tailwater that fishes well at a hundred cubic feet per second was cranked up well past a thousand, and a few of us drove up there—without fishing tackle—just to look at it.

Some local guides had their clients dredging nymphs and split shot along the swollen banks of streams where they'd normally be casting size 16 caddis flies. A few beginners thought this was just what fly-fishing is like, while others knew the score but were happy enough to be fishing for trout in beautiful surroundings. But there weren't many of either, and some outfitters watched the better part of a year's worth of bookings wash downstream with the high water. It was the last thing they needed in the middle of what some journalists were calling the Great Recession.

One day in July, I ducked under a locked Forest Service gate and hiked a mile up the closed road to a trailhead on the edge of a nearby wilderness area. Once there I strapped on the snowshoes I'd carried in and headed up to a lake I know at 10,400 feet. I quickly lost the trail under fifteen-foot snowdrifts, but I didn't think I'd need it. I knew I had to work my way up and west into a large cirque and then, at a point I assumed I'd recognize, cut north, drop into a willow-choked creek bottom, ford the stream and continue on through a stand of krummholz to the small lake.

This was an experiment. I'd never been up there in deep snow before, and I wasn't sure that the lake was thawed or if the stream would be low enough to cross, even at the usual shallow spot. But it worked out okay. I missed the ford by a few hundred yards—the snow cover made everything look different—but once I spotted the creek, I knew where I was and easily backtracked. I waded across the creek with exaggerated care, using a stick for balance and carrying the snowshoes under my free arm. The water was ice-cold, and I understood that if I went in I'd be hypothermic in seconds and several miles through deep snow from the truck.

The lake was open except for a hundred-foot stretch of the south shore where a snow bank hung a twelve-foot-high, windblown cornice out over the water. There were still a few miniature icebergs in the water, as well as the spreading rings from a handful of feeding trout. When I'd left the house that morning, it was sunny and around eighty degrees. Up there it was lightly overcast, breezy and in the low sixties. Before stringing up my rod, I put on the wool sweater and fleece vest I'd carried in the pack.

I discovered this lake sometime in the 1970s. Of course, it was known to some, including whoever originally stocked nonnative brook trout in it, but it's well out of sight of the trail that leads to the larger lake above it and it's off-channel, so you could miss it even if you were fishing up the creek. It's really just a permanent four- or five-acre pothole fed by snowmelt and spring seeps, but it's rich in midges, scuds and small caddis, and supports a population of feral brook trout. And to this day it doesn't appear on any map I've seen of the area.

I fished a small hare's ear and partridge soft hackle that afternoon and landed eight or nine trout, the largest between twelve and fourteen inches. The brookies here have always been unusually gorgeous, possibly because the breeding season is so early at this altitude that they just stay in spawning colors all year long. In this drab, wintry landscape, they were so brilliant they seemed to be lit from the inside.

On the hike out I convinced myself that I was the first to fish the lake that year. After all, the ice couldn't have been off for long and the only tracks I saw were the ones I made coming in. Of course, there are plenty of fishermen around who know these mountains well—a whole generation of them more intrepid than I am—and their tracks could have been erased by sun and wind in a matter of days. But the story I'm sticking to is that I was the first.

Less than a week later, I was back up there with a friend I'll call Tom, who by then was living in my spare bedroom. The fish weren't quite as eager that day, but we caught a few and Tom saw but didn't hook one he guessed at sixteen inches. As a lifelong Michigan fisherman, he has a soft spot for brook trout, and he said he'd never seen anything prettier than this little lake nestled among stunted Engelmann spruce and subalpine fir under snow-capped, 12,000-foot peaks.

Tom was one of the over 15 million Americans who were out of work that year, all with depressingly similar stories. He'd been without a job for several years in a state with an official unemployment rate of 16 percent. (When I asked what he did all that time, he said, a little cryptically, I thought, "I fished every day in season, but not always *all day*.") Finally he got a job here in Colorado and relocated, arriving with a U-Haul trailer towed by a preposterously ratty old Toyota with a Michigan plate on the back and an expired New Mexico plate in front. He was all but broke by then, and I lent him money for rent and car repairs (which he paid back out of his first paycheck), although he managed to scrape together $56 on his own to buy a nonresident season fishing license. He could have waited six months to establish residency, but that would have cost him half a year's worth of fishing.

But by the time we hiked up to the lake, Tom had been laid off from the new job (last hired, first fired) and had lost his house in Michigan to foreclosure. When he had to leave the room he was renting because that house was also foreclosed on, it was largely a formality, since he could no longer afford rent anyway. That's when I told him to move in with me. He agreed only because it was either that or sleep in his car. I was happy to do it and happy to be *able* to do it. After all, thirty-five or forty years ago you wouldn't have picked me out of my crowd as the guy who'd one day be stable and solvent enough to come to for help. Through it all he continued to look for steady work, did whatever odd jobs he could pick up and went fishing whenever he had a day off or even just a few free hours. He was like a kid in a candy store with a whole state full of new trout streams to explore. When I mentioned that it was a shame about the high runoff he simply said, "Well, shit happens."

All of which is to say, those of us whose worst problem that summer was finding good places to fish didn't feel we had much room to complain.

The four of us, Doug, Chris, Vince and I, finally made it to Montana in September and ended up staying at a modest lodge that looked, from a distance, like a sprawling 1950s vintage motel. It had a large dining room with picture windows looking west across the valley toward the massive bulk of the Pioneer Mountains. The sunsets were spectacularly orange as the last rays filtered through the smoke from nearby wildfires and flocks of sandhill cranes glided by on their prehistoric errands.

We went to the Big Hole, where our guide, Graham, said the fishing had been slow, but the river was clear and lovely, with pods of lazily rising trout here and there in long slicks and the tails of riffles. The trout did seem reticent: ignoring some flies and mouthing others as if they'd woken up with hangovers and were halfheartedly picking at breakfast. These are the slow-motion takes that are guaranteed to make a tightly wound fisherman miss the set. So to slow ourselves down, we sank into the quiet luxury of fishing a beautiful river from the comfort of a drift boat with a competent young guide at the oars. It was a few hours into a perfect day with a deep blue sky filled with hawks and grasshoppers clicking in the grass below the railroad bed. Graham was relaxed and talkative, having determined that the two clients in his boat weren't the best fly casters he'd ever seen, but they didn't seem to be fish hogs or assholes.

In the end, some trout were caught and I even managed to break a rod on a big, heavy rainbow. He followed a streamer out from a grassy bank, and as he got close to the boat, I went into a fast scissor trip, sweeping the rod one way and the line hand the other to speed up the fly. This is the only way I know to induce a strike from a following fish. By the time the trout took and turned, the rod was far back over my shoulder, and when I set hard it snapped at the ferrule with a loud crack. There was a perplexing split second as one hemisphere of my brain wondered what that noise was and why the rod had gone limp while the other knew exactly what had happened. I once went for a period of over twenty years of hard fishing and broke only one rod. I've now broken four in the last five years, but wondering why that might be is not a profitable way to direct your thinking.

The Beaverhead River was livelier. Even before the chill had left the air in the morning, the craneflies would appear, fluttering and bouncing over the water like giant, gangly mosquitoes. I have an indelible mental image from the first morning. We were anchored at a good run waiting for the morning mist to clear when Jesse, our guide, pointed and said, "There's a cranefly." At that moment a chubby brown trout leapt from the water in a perfect parabolic arc, nailed the fly a foot above the river and seemed to hang there for the longest time before falling with a splash.

Jesse had a cranefly pattern he liked—spent wings and an extended foam body on a size 12 hook—but the key was action. It wasn't possible to imitate accurately the behavior of these bugs, but a halting, high-stick skitter would sometimes be close enough, and when it was, the strikes were vicious.

Later in the day we'd drift hoppers and droppers along the banks, switching first one pattern and then the other until we lit on a combination that worked for a while. When it stopped working, we'd start all over again. In late summer and fall, a western guide's arsenal leans heavily on hoppers—large and small, drab and bright, bushy and trim, fur and feathers or foam and rubber—enough patterns to keep two fishermen busy changing flies all though a lazy afternoon.

Still later, as evening came on, we'd switch to heavier rods and fish streamers, slapping them as far up under the overhanging willows as possible and stripping them out so fast we got rope burns on our fingers from the lines. You could think a slower retrieve would give the fish an easier shot at the fly, but in fact the sight of fleeing prey triggers strikes and it's not humanly possible to strip a fly so fast that a trout that wants it can't catch it. Or as a friend says of streamer fishing, "When in doubt, rip it out."

Neither the Big Hole nor the Beaverhead was unusually crowded, but with the rivers finally low and clear there were lots of fishermen around, busily coming and going in bars and fly shops and rumbling up and down the back roads towing all manner of drift boats, including a homemade plywood number outside of Twin Bridges that looked like a coffin with oarlocks.

It was the usual mix of western river personnel. There were trout bums sleeping in vans and referring to the Beaverhead as "the Beave," family men on vacation, working stiffs with more tools than tackle in the beds of their pickups, natty sports with pressed shirts and blocked felt hats and the odd bond trader with a trophy wife: one of those women who, like some house cats, make it by being decorative but don't catch many mice.

One evening when we came in, we told the lodge owner we wanted to fish till dark the next day—missing dinner at the lodge—and then buy the guides burgers and a few beers afterward. (We'd already cleared this with the guides and they were all for it.) But the owner said no, the guides worked for him and he insisted on having all his people back at seven-thirty for supper. "His people." The guides were looking down, apparently studying the gravel they were standing on. The rest of us glanced at each other, wondering if this was worth throwing a hissy fit over and deciding it wasn't.

Back home in Colorado the season petered out gradually. Some rivers did finally come down, and as often happens in high-water years, the trout were well fed and rested and the fishing was glorious for the few weeks it lasted, with the days short and cool; the cottonwoods, willows and dogwoods in fall colors; and the sky filled with Canada geese. It was the full enchilada.

Other streams, especially the small creeks up in the high country, never warmed up enough for the hatches to come off and were still in the last stages of runoff when the nights turned cold enough for the first frosts. It was possible to nymph up a trout or two to prove a point, but for the first time in thirty-five years, there was no dry-fly season at all on my favorite no-longer-quite-so-secret mountain stream.

Tom finally landed a job on the Gulf Coast of Florida. It wasn't exactly what he was hoping for and he wasn't happy about moving so far away from trout fishing, but it was paying work, so he took it anyway. He left right ahead of the first big snowstorm in late October and drove south into Texas before turning east, hoping to keep his bald tires on dry roads. I was worried about him, but he managed to get his old car through seven states without breaking down or having the police stop him to ask about the mismatched license plates. He called when he got there to say that he'd never fished salt water before, but was eager to try it.

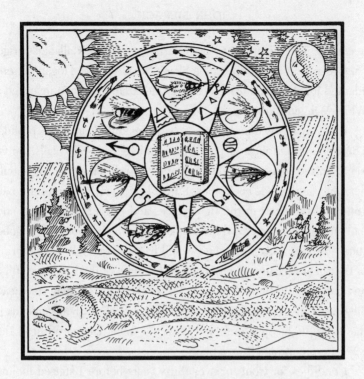

16

THE NUCLEAR OPTION

The other day I showed some steelhead flies I'd tied and that I was cautiously proud of to a friend from Washington State. He said, "These are no good." Susan, who can sometimes be sweetly naïve, gave me a knowing look. She now understands that this kind of gruff irony is what passes as a compliment among some men, although she may never understand why.

These were the kind of fancy patterns that some steelheaders swear by and that others say are pretty enough to look at but aren't

necessary. There were some Spey variations of Dan Callahan's original Green Butt Skunk and some Skagit Mists—a Dec Hogan pattern
adapted for steelhead from a century-old Atlantic salmon fly called a
White-Winged Akroyd.

Every fly tier will understand what I mean by "cautiously proud."
These were complicated patterns complete with tags, tails, butts,
joints, mixed blue-eared pheasant and gadwall hackle, goose shoulder wings and jungle cock sides. I'd worked slowly and carefully, had
gotten all the parts in the right places and proper proportions and
had managed not to crowd the heads, all of which amounts to a good
start. The flies looked okay and would fish well enough, but in terms
of the sheer elegance that's achieved by some tiers, they were still a
few degrees off plumb. The very best of these classic-style steelhead
flies aren't just beautiful; they also seem thoughtlessly organic, as if
the entire fly has just unfolded from the small, lacquered head the
way a flower sprouts from a bud.

I tied flies for trout for over thirty years before I started fooling
around with steelhead patterns, and the idea of tying patterns for fish
that weren't eating stumped me at first. This is the kind of unsolv-
able puzzle that, like religion, causes some to settle on a comforting
homeliness and turns others into flaming visionaries, each according
to his own nature.

That would explain why one experienced steelheader carries elegant, feather-winged wet flies dripping with golden pheasant, ostrich
and jungle cock and the next has a box full of unadorned marabou
powder puffs. The natural exuberance of fly tiers explains why there
are so many patterns to choose from, including those brainstorms a
guide friend calls "three-beer flies." If the tier happens to have the
TV on in the background at the moment of creation, these things can
end up looking like the radioactive octopus from a late night horror
movie.

In fact, there's a convincing argument in steelheading that it's all about presentation and that beyond basic considerations of large or small and bright or dark, fly pattern hardly matters. This leads some tiers to say that since pattern doesn't matter, you might as well just lash some rabbit fur to a hook and be done with it. Others conclude, with equal conviction, that since pattern doesn't matter, you might as well get a pile of exotic feathers and knock yourself out. It comes down to personality. To a certain kind of tier, letting go of any amount of beauty in the interest of practicality is agonizing, while to another practicality *is* beauty. I've learned to decisively keep a foot in each camp based on a comment by novelist and steelhead fisherman Thomas McGuane. He agreed that it probably *is* all about presentation, but added, "The trouble is, you can't properly present something you don't believe in."

So maybe the right fly is the one that not only fools a fish every now and then, but also fools the fisherman into keeping it in the water long enough for that to happen—if not actually believing in every cast and swing, then at least not becoming despondent. Think of it as the angling equivalent of the placebo effect. My friend Scott Sadil said, "If you're changing flies while steelheading, you're in a slump." Someone else once said, "The most important thing in steelhead fishing is confidence—I think."

This business of presentation versus pattern is the longest-running argument in fly-fishing. It will never be settled because for every day when it seems to be all about presentation, there's another day when it seems to be all about presentation *of the right fly*. Of course trout fishing has the advantage of being somewhat empirical. All things being equal, a trout fly that's drifted properly through the right water for an hour without a strike begins to look like the wrong fly for that time and place. Steelheading is more faith-based. A steelhead fly that you've fished for three days without a pull could still turn out to be the right one.

And then there's the idea of the comeback fly, one of the most arcane concepts in steelheading. This is the term of art for the fly you change to when a fish has swirled at or halfheartedly bumped the fly you're fishing, indicating that he might be willing to play, but not with that pattern. For most the comeback fly is something smaller, darker and sparser than whatever they were fishing—sometimes so sparse it's just a little wisp of a thing that looks as if it had been left unfinished. For some fishermen the comeback fly is always different, determined by whatever they were fishing that brought up the player in the first place. For others it's a specific pattern, maybe tied in a couple of sizes to reflect conditions.

I once asked a steelheader in Oregon, "If your comeback fly is so effective, why not just fish it all the time?"

He explained that the bigger, flashier fly would attract the attention of more fish and even hook some of them, while the comeback fly was reserved for the tough customers. "It's the steak and potatoes that gets him in the door," he said, "but it's that little piece of cheesecake that closes the deal."

Since I started steelheading, I've managed to fill three boxes with flies: an odd assortment of this and that pattern as I became aware of them through guides and friends. I've fished some of them and have actually caught steelhead on a precious few. (Among the ones that worked are some patterns I didn't especially like at first, but then nothing makes a goofy fly look beautiful like catching a fish on it.) I've also picked up a little knowledge of the sport along the way, including the inescapable fact that three boxes crammed with steelhead flies is the mark of an amateur.

Most of the experienced steelheaders I've met carry a single, small box containing what seems like a meager selection of flies. There was a young guide on the Deschutes River who had a few neat rows of flawlessly tied classic wets, any one of which could have been framed and hung convincingly on the wall. When I complimented him on his tying, he shrugged and said he didn't know if it made a difference or not but "there's just something about showing the fish your best effort." There was also a well-known steelheader on the North Umpqua who, on that particular day, had exactly seven flies in his box, all wildly mismatched and all looking like they'd been retrieved from bankside branches or submerged rocks, as I suspect they had.

Granted, these guys' boxes might have looked different in another season with changes in water temperature, depth and clarity (steelhead flies tend to get bigger and darker as the rivers do the same), but the message was still clear: Get some flies you like, stay faithful to them and work on your casting.

One of the things that drew me to the elaborate, full-dress steelhead patterns is their contrast with the drab, practical trout flies I usually tie. Even some of the simplest steelhead hair-wings have a few fussy little architectural touches because anadromous fish are thought to be suckers for visual complexity. And if a little bit of gingerbread works, why not go the full distance with flying buttresses and blind arches? This is sometimes referred to as the Fallacy of Wishful Thinking, but knowing what it's called doesn't mean you can't fall victim to it. I've always liked flies that are plain and workmanlike, but it seems encoded in the human condition that as soon as you achieve simplicity in one area of life, you're likely to go all Victorian in another.

This is the impulse that causes some tiers to build those lovely and possibly pointless full-dress Atlantic salmon flies: the ones that will see the light of day only from a shadow-box frame and that will never, ever get wet. I tried my hand at some of these once as an exercise in something or other, but didn't get very far. I tended to overdress the flies—forgetting back at the tag, tail and butt that there were seven more operations to go before I started on the wing. And then my married wings themselves—not unlike some of my friends— wouldn't *stay* married for reasons that were never clear.

It's possible that I just wasn't a good-enough tier, but I think the real reason was a lack of immediacy. I manage to freeload myself into decent Atlantic salmon fishing only once a decade on average, and when I do go, I use the simpler, hair-winged flies that are now standard. In other words, when there isn't a fish somewhere in the deal, I lose interest.

I overdressed my steelhead flies at first, too, even though I knew they were supposed to be sparse. (A friend said of my first batch, "They're nice enough, but don't quit your day job.") Even the simplest hair-wing, like a Purple Peril, can get clunky in the wrong hands and the potential gets greater as patterns get more complex. When you sit down to tie something like a Skagit Mist, the question becomes, how do you tie a fly with eleven separate materials and fourteen distinct anatomical parts that still has the requisite air and light that a painter would call "negative space"? Turns out you do it with a sharp eye toward proportion and a sense that everything needs room to breathe.

Aside from the aesthetic prescription, there are also some engineering considerations. For instance, the long, dangly heron substitute hackle on a spey pattern should be tied sparsely because steelhead are said to like it that way, but also because too much hackle underneath counterbalanced only by that skinny, low-set wing on top can cause the fly to roll on its side in the current, ruining the silhouette. Which begs the question, Do steelhead really prefer sparsely tied spey flies, or are the sparsely tied flies the only ones they get a decent look at?

And don't even get me started on hooks. Even if you stick with the traditional japanned black, up-eye salmon hooks, there are too many choices. I lean toward the Alec Jackson spey hook because it holds well, makes a graceful fly and its medium wire nicely splits the difference. But then there are days when you want a fly to wake or skate on the surface and other days when you want it to all but plow gravel on the swing. Naturally, there's a selection of specialized hooks for each purpose and they can cost as much as a dollar each.

It took me the better part of three decades to pare my core trout-fly selection down to a generous handful of mostly simple, straight-forward patterns. I'm thinking that having learned that lesson once; it won't take me nearly as long with steelhead flies. On the other hand, there are certain phases you have to go through—like puberty—so you might as well get on with it.

Once you tumble for the fancy steelhead flies in the picture books, you're sunk. Even as you tell yourself you can just admire them from afar like works of art, you know in your heart that you'll eventually have to tie some and fish them as part of your ongoing education. If you're like me, you'll envy those who can tie on a steel-head fly with the offhanded confidence of a DEA agent slapping a fresh clip into his 9-millimeter while you dither over the black one, the purple one or that pretty little orange one. You'll develop your own preferences eventually, but you also have your pride as a tier and don't want to limit yourself to flies you're not afraid to tie.

There's also the single drawback to being a fly tier, which is that you like to tie flies and can find it hard to stop. I fish enough to burn through my favorite trout patterns at a pretty good clip, but unless you're a complete klutz—and we all have our moments—you just don't lose a lot of steelhead flies, so they can begin to pile up. Eventually you may have to reconcile the flies you want to tie with the ones you actually need to catch fish.

In an attempt to imitate those who know what they're doing (not a bad fishing strategy, by the way), I now limit myself to a single fly box on the river. It's a big old Wheatley salmon box with a swing leaf and 110 clips, but it's still just the one box—and no one has to know how many flies I have stashed in my luggage.

It's become my secret ambition to someday design a steelhead fly that's so effective I can call it the Nuclear Option, but so far I've mostly stuck with established patterns. There's no science that I can see behind steelhead flies—or if there is, it's the kind of science that would have felt at home in the Dark Ages—but I'm hoping there's a kind of alchemy in operation that you don't have to understand in order to copy. It's also easier this way. When you start trying to invent patterns, it's possible to spend a pleasant evening tying steelhead flies, only to wake up screaming in the middle of the night at the thought that you should have veiled your blue-eared pheasant hackle with orange-dyed mallard instead of natural.

Confidence in your fly pattern really is important in steelheading, and you take confidence where you find it. If a guide or local hotshot points at a fly in your box and says, "Try that," or, better yet, gives you a fly of his own, you'd be a fool not to fish it. Failing that, you glance at the river, open your fly box and wait for inspiration. The right fly will be like a Tibetan prayer flag to those of us who are not practicing Buddhists. It may or may not bring good fortune as promised, but it can't hurt and it looks real pretty.

17

ADLATOK

My salmon guide on the Adlatok River was a man named Jordan
Locke. We'd met and fished together on one of my previous trips to
Labrador and I knew him to be hell on brook trout, but he'd made
it clear even then that his real expertise was Atlantic salmon. He
told some wild stories about his salmon trips in Newfoundland that I
chose to believe. That's partly because when you're fishing for some
of the biggest brook trout in the world you'll believe anything, but
also because, in my experience, Newfoundlanders are reliably honest.

These are not only inherently good-hearted people, but as a practical matter many of them live in small, insular communities where bullshitters are always caught out in the end.

Jordan has all the attributes of a good guide, including the most important one of really wanting you to catch fish. If he didn't like you, I don't think he could hide it convincingly, but it wouldn't make a difference. He'd still be deeply invested in your success as a matter of professional pride. I could also understand him, which made things easier. Some of these guides have such thick accents that they might as well be speaking Gaelic. Given time and repetition, I could work out that, for instance, "trimmer ook" was Newfie for "streamer hook," but in day-to-day conversation I was often reduced to smiling and nodding like an idiot.

The only thing that makes me nervous about Jordan is that he's a rock hopper. I mean that he leaps around these boulder-strewn rivers like Rudolf Nureyev, either forgetting or not caring that we're hundreds of miles by floatplane from the nearest place where you could get a broken bone set. He's young, agile and sure-footed as a goat, but over the long haul the odds seem against him.

I remember some grainy cellphone footage of Jordan netting a fish. He's seen high-stepping at a dead run through a knee-deep riffle, going down hard and coming up dripping wet with a brook trout that weighed eight pounds in the net—the brook trout of a lifetime for the client who'd hooked it. There was some discussion about this back at the lodge. Jordan claimed it was an intentional diving catch, but some others thought it looked like an accidental fall topped off with a miraculous save. My feeling was, as long as he came up with the fish in the net, it was Jordan who deserved to make the call.

There are only two good pools on this stretch of the Adlatok, each with steep rapids above and below and lying just upstream from tidewater on the North Atlantic. We came on them along a high ridge that gave us almost an aerial view and stopped for that first long look.

There's no telling what will go through your mind at this moment: confidence, dread of failure, or sheer amazement at having gotten this far. So many expedition-grade fishing trips begin and end as idle talk, joining the exercise machines, language tapes and other self-improvement schemes that never quite panned out. Why one plan withers on the vine and the next puts you four travel days and twenty five hundred miles from home on the ragged-ass coast of Labrador is a complete mystery.

We climbed down to the Presidential Pool, named for former president George H. W. Bush, who had once fished it. Two years earlier I'd fished another Presidential Pool named for the same senior Bush on the Tree River in Nunavut, and I wondered briefly if I'd done something karmically disastrous and was now fated to spend the rest of my life breathing the exhaust of this elderly Republican.

This was the kind of sublime pool salmon fishers see when they lean back in their office chairs and close their eyes. It sat in a shallow gorge of weathered rock with a fringe of black spruce at the top: low, dark, tight-needled trees that gave the impression of holding on for dear life. The pool itself was the size of a small mountain lake. It was deep, clear, braided and foamy at the head and with a glassy tailout where dozens of salmon were fining lazily. They looked half asleep as holding fish do, but now and then one would detach itself from the pod and jump before backing down and parking in its original spot. Experts disagree about why the salmon do this. Some say it's to loosen the eggs, others claim it's to shake off sea lice, and still others say it's pure exuberance, that salmon jump simply because they can. It's a question that has troubled great minds for centuries.

We waded in along a sheer granite cliff and went to work. Jordan looked in my fly box, picked out a size 8 Green Machine and tied it on with a riffling hitch. On the third skating swing, a salmon rose calmly from the bottom to look at the fly, backed down with it for an inch as we held our breath, and then turned away. The fish showed no further curiosity after several more swings, so we tried a little Brown Bomber with an orange butt, a Copper Killer and then a Blue Charm, all of which the fish did a good job of ignoring.

I was beginning to feel stumped, but only a fool walks away from an interested salmon. I asked if we should rest the fish, but Jordan said no, picked out a smaller Green Machine—a size 12—and tied it on. He's one of those guides who insist on tying up your terminal tackle even if you'd prefer to do it yourself. His reasoning goes without saying. There's a better than even chance that Atlantic salmon won't bite, and even if one does, much of what happens next is out of his control. If a client flubs the set or plays the fish poorly, there's not much he can do about it, but Jordan is not about to have his best efforts ruined by inept knot tying.

On the first swing with the little Green Machine, the fish rose up and casually inhaled the fly as if that was the one he'd been waiting for. When I set, he jumped as high as my head and I bowed to the fish, dropping the rod tip so he wouldn't land on the tight leader and break it when he came down. Then there was a long run and another jump near the top of the pool, far enough away that I had to remind myself it was my fish. I bowed again and the fish stayed on. I was fighting back an escalating sense of panic. Jordan leaned casually on his long-handled net and said, "I guess they likes green, ey?"

I first learned about this river when I talked to my friend Robin Reeve, owner of Three Rivers Lodge in Labrador, back in January. He told me about an Atlantic salmon camp on the Adlatok that was for sale for what the current owner described as "any offer that isn't an insult." The place had been abandoned for ten years, the guy was eager to unload it and Robin was cautiously tempted. Exactly *why* it had been abandoned for ten years is the first question I asked. Robin said the guy had been vague, but that the list of things that can go sideways at a remote wilderness camp is a long one with bankruptcy and burnout both near the top.

Robin isn't a salmon fisherman himself, but he thought this might make a nice fly-out camp for the few weeks late in the season when the salmon were in the river in good numbers and, coincidentally, when the brook trout fishing closer to the lodge was beginning to wind down. He also thought there'd be a neat aesthetic fit, since fishing for trophy brook trout and Atlantic salmon both redefine success outside the usual numbers game.

All Robin knew about the Adlatok was that Lee Wulff once described it as "a crown jewel," that the fish there were said to have a weakness for skated flies and that the height of the season was in early August. That's when he thought we should fly out and take a look at it.

He said, "You fish for Atlantic salmon, right?"

"I *have* fished for them," I answered, carefully not claiming to be the consultant who could properly evaluate this fishery from a business perspective, but not exactly denying it, either.

The camp was out on the coast, roughly 360 miles round-trip from the lodge and well out of range of the de Havilland Beaver floatplane crammed with gear and provisions. Bush pilots calculate fuel by figuring the distance to be traveled, eyeballing the load and then adding something like a half hour's worth of slop in either direction to allow for headwinds, detours around weather and such. Half an hour each way cuts it close for my taste. Once, while driving across Wyoming, I inadvertently ran my tank down to fumes and got pretty nervous, but even if the worst had happened, my pickup wouldn't have plummeted out of the sky.

But even with the most generous estimate, a full tank in the Beaver would get us there and only halfway back. So a week or two earlier when the plane could be spared from the usual daily fly-outs from the lodge, Robin and the pilot, Gilles, had flown out halfway and stashed a load of aviation gas on the shore of a handy lake for a refueling stop. This was a time-consuming and expensive errand—like everything else in this country—but Robin really wanted to get out to the Adlatok.

The flight to the river was long, but uneventful as these things go. The gas was where it had been left in five-gallon jerry cans, so we topped off the tank and took the rest with us, cracking the windows to vent the fumes. Closer to the coast we flew into the kind of low, broken overcast pilots call "scud," and at one point Gilles put us right on the deck to duck under a squall rather than waste fuel flying around it. And then near the mouth of the river, there was a moment of confusion as we circled looking for the camp. The roofs of some wilderness camps are painted red or orange so they can be easily spotted from the air, but not this one. But then there it was, more or less where it was supposed to be. After a pass upriver to make sure the water was deep enough and there were no obstructions, Gilles landed and taxied to the beach.

There had once been a dock, but after a decade of neglect, wind and shifting ice, there was nothing left but the pilings, so we waded ashore and tied the plane to a sturdy alder. The camp was in no better shape. Bears had torn up two of the four plywood cabins foraging for food; a third was doorless, windowless and ankle-deep in dead bats; the storage shed stood open to the weather with the door hanging by one hinge. We stashed our gear in the one cabin that was still more or less intact, and while Robin and Gilles swept up dead flies and mouse turds and otherwise tried to make the place livable, I headed for the pools with Jordan.

The camp's fiberglass canoe was still serviceable, but the outboard had been left with gas in the tank that after ten years had turned the consistency of asphalt. We managed to locate some old paddles that weren't too badly dry-rotted and paddled downstream through a mile of frog water to the head of the first rapids, where we beached the boat. From there it was nearly another mile to the pools over steep rock ledges, thick spruce woods and alder thickets humming with black flies. The owner had told Robin it was an easy fifteen-minute stroll from the camp to the pools. Maybe he remembered it wrong.

When we got back that first evening, I reported that I'd landed two salmon and hooked and lost a third that I was still secretly stewing over. I tried to invoke my better self by quoting Izaak Walton's dictum "No man can lose what he never had," but my true self kept interrupting with, "Damn it, that was my fish!" Robin and Gilles had spruced up the cabin nicely. It was still a borderline ruin, but the worst of the crap had been swept out, sleeping bags and pads had been placed on the floor between the stains where the roof had leaked and they'd managed to get the propane stove going so there was coffee on. Some of the screens were still in the windows, but a missing chunk of wall off the kitchen big enough to drive a truck through made the screens a moot point, so several mosquito coils were smoldering to keep the bugs at bay. All in all, it was real homey.

The next morning I tried the bottom pool for a while. I'd seen a salmon roll down there the day before, but what I really liked about it was its open back cast. Standing in front of the granite face at the Presidential Pool, I could manage an adequate cast with the 13½-foot spey rod, but I was paranoid about ticking my fly on that rock. Ted Leeson once said that hooking a salmon on a fly "borders on religious experience and happens about as often," so if you missed a take only to learn that you'd been fishing with a hookless fly, shooting yourself would be your only real option.

In the course of three passes with three different flies—a Green Machine, a Black Bear Green Butt and a Green Highlander—I decided I didn't like this run after all. It had looked good from a distance, but up close the current seemed too fast and there was nothing I could bring myself to believe in as holding water. The fish I'd seen rolling may have just been moving through, and it's an article of faith that traveling fish won't take. Still, I fished out all three passes diligently, fussing over the drift and following the best advice I ever got on anadromous fish by starting higher in the pool than I thought I should and swinging farther into the tail than I thought was necessary. Jordan had stayed upstream with Robin, leaving me to tie my own knots. This was either a vote of confidence or simply the realization that he couldn't be in two places at once.

Back at the Presidential Pool a salmon refused my Black Bear Green Butt, coming so close that the fly rose on a transparent bulge of water with a silvery fish shape visible inside. I was still staring at this heartbreakingly empty hole in the water as the fly swung down into the lip of the rapids, where another, larger salmon rolled on it heading downstream and came tight. Since he was facing into the white water anyway, he just continued in that direction. I'd been afraid of this. The rapids stretched for eighty yards into the next run and the bank was a jumble of polished, furniture-sized boulders that it had taken me fifteen minutes to pick my way through when I went down there earlier. It was a prescription for a lost fish.

It all speeds up from there. The salmon ran down the rapids tearing line off the reel. I had the regulation 250 yards of braided Dacron behind my spey line, but once a fish is out of the pool and into the backing, every turn of the reel increases the likelihood of disaster. I could feel the weight of the current and the oceanic strength of the salmon through the long rod and it all seemed hopeless. But then the fish ducked into an eddy behind a rock along the near bank. I was stumbling downstream as fast as possible, focused on the salmon and my unsure footing, so I only caught a peripheral image of Jordan bouncing across those boulders the way you'd skip a flat rock across a pond, landing in the eddy with a splash and coming up with a goofy grin and a silver torpedo. I wasn't entirely sure what had just happened, but my fly was in the salmon's jaw and the salmon was in the net, which is all that counts in the end.

Robin didn't buy the camp. He wasn't bothered by the condition of the place—for the few weeks a year he'd need it he could tear down the cabins and pitch wall tents—and he didn't care that much of the stuff on the inventory he'd been given was either trashed or missing. It was more a matter of daunting logistics. Floatplanes are hideously expensive to operate in the best of circumstances, and the extra flight halfway out and back to stash fuel for each trip would push the cost over the top.

You'd want to keep the plane with you at the salmon camp anyway. It would be too expensive to shuttle it back and forth and you'd need it there in case the weather abruptly turned snarky on the coast and you had to make a quick getaway. Otherwise you could have a party of fishermen stranded out there for weeks. But then it would also be needed for daily fly-outs back at the lodge, so your only alternative would be to lease a second plane and hire another pilot for the short salmon season, piling that expense onto the already staggering fuel cost. It's true that people sometimes pay obscene amounts of money to fish for Atlantic salmon, but there's still a practical limit.

The dearth of fishable water was another drawback. There was really just the Presidential Pool, and although it was a big, cosmic honey hole, a certain kind of client would quickly tire of fishing that one spot.

We did wonder if there was more good water in the hundred river miles upstream, but we didn't have enough fuel to go exploring and if anyone knew anything they were keeping it quiet. Later, when I asked an outfitter out of Schefferville, Quebec, if there was any salmon fishing on the Adlatok inland from the coast, he gave the kind of concisely laconic answer you get used to in Labrador: "Some says yes; some says no. Me? I thinks no."

We'd seen some good-looking pools from the air on the way in, but they were down in a narrow canyon, and Gilles said they'd be death traps to get in and out of in a fixed-wing aircraft. A full heli-copter expedition—complete with fuel and provision drops along the way—would take weeks and cost more than a college education.

We hadn't talked about it for more than a few minutes when I realized that none of us would ever see this river again.

18

KLICKITAT

One October, while taking a break between passes through a pool on the Klickitat River in Washington State, Jeff Cottrell said to me, "I think you've become a steelheader." I took it as a compliment, even though I didn't really know what he meant. Probably just that I'd worked the entire run methodically, starting higher than some would and fishing so far into the tail that the fly ticked gravel on my last swing. Or maybe, in a more general sense, that I'd simply learned to embrace the monotony without losing hope. There's a higher step on this path where you actually come to *crave* the monotony the way skydivers crave adrenaline, but that level of enlightenment is still somewhere in my future.

My friends and I *do* occasionally take breaks while steelheading, although not everyone does. If there's one thing all steelhead fishers agree on, it's that your odds of catching fish are invariably slim, but they increase the longer you keep a hook in the water. There's a lot more to it than just putting in time, but that's what you start with and it's what you return to when all else fails. There's the story of a local steelheader who's so persistent that he'll pee in his waders rather than stop casting for five minutes to wade ashore and take care of business in the normal way. It's said that he stinks from stewing in his own juices, but he's widely admired for his purity of intent.

From the first time I went steelhead fishing, I had the sense of being sunk in these kinds of clichés. It's not just that steelhead are hard to catch—plenty of fish are hard to catch—it's that they don't feed in any recognizable way when they return to their home rivers to spawn, so they're not really supposed to bite. But then they do bite every once in a while—not often, by a long shot, but more often than you'd think, given that it shouldn't happen at all.

No one knows why, although there are plenty of guesses. It could be latent instinct, idle nibbling, curiosity, playfulness or anger—the states of mind we extrapolate from the way a fish takes or boils at a fly—although my own theory is that it's something impenetrable to the mammalian mind. Pondering this as you cast and step down run after run without a strike eventually gets under your skin. You don't feel crazy, but you begin to think you must be.

Scott Sadil said this could become such an exercise in futility that when you do finally hook a steelhead after days or weeks of casting, you don't feel relief or elation, but instead think, Okay, now something can *really* go wrong. Another friend lives in the heart of steelhead country in Oregon, but only fishes for trout. He says, reasonably enough, "I like to catch a fish every once in a while."

It's impossible to explain the attraction except to say that steelheading is like golf: viewed objectively, it makes no sense, but some people like it. Whatever the reason, when you become a steelheader, you've either joined an elite class of anglers with heightened sensibilities or you've entered the lunatic fringe of a periphery: a place were voluntarily peeing in your waders indicates a strong work ethic.

Because of the kind of mind I was born with, I didn't come at steelheading straight on, but sidled up to it sideways. At first it was an excuse to spey-cast with long, two-handed rods. Later it became a pretext to tie those pretty steelhead flies I'd otherwise have no use for. I was consciously trying to develop an acquired taste and did catch a few steelhead along the way. They were undeniably sweet fish that came one at a time after great effort, but I wasn't sure they entirely lived up to the hype. Then a friend said that although all steelhead are steelhead, it's only the occasional bruiser that really cleans your clock, which only put the carrot on a longer stick.

I *had* begun to see that the long dead spaces that drive bottom-line types nuts were like waiting for Christmas knowing it doesn't come every day, but it was only on my fourth or fifth trip that I began to see the light. Toward the end of a nearly fishless week in March on the North Umpqua, I abruptly found myself stumbling down the slippery right bank trying to keep up with a fourteen-pound wild hen on her way back to the ocean with most of my backing. I thought, in an oddly calm way, This fish is pretty damned strong.

There were four of us fishing that October: Doug, Vince and I, who'd driven out from Colorado, and Jeff, who at the time ran a fly shop in The Dalles, Oregon—a town poignantly named after a set of rapids that's now flooded by a dam on the Columbia. Jeff and his wife, Jan, had been putting us up at their house for the last few days while we fished the Deschutes with Scott and two off-duty guides named Leif and Nate. Then Jeff took some time off to fish with us on the Klickitat.

By that I mean he closed the shop and taped a handwritten GONE FISHING sign in the window. That's something every fisherman will defer to, even a disappointed customer who needs a spool of tippet on his way to the river. There's deep respect among anglers for the neat trick of making a living from fishing while still appreciating it as more than just a job. It's also a paradox worthy of the sport that the guy you want to buy your gear from is precisely the guy who might be off fishing during what the rest of the world thinks of as business hours.

For the first few days on the Klickitat, I experienced the usual sensory overload from new water. There was the sheer beauty of the river that anyone could see, as well as the particular shapes of the water and my imperfect knowledge of how fish might fit themselves between rocks, depth, current and shade. Fishermen love rivers for their own sake, but we always look at them with the knowledge that it can take years to begin to see what's actually there. That's why we can't take our eyes off them. I've been in cars that almost crashed because the driver and all the passengers were looking at a river instead of the road.

Jeff wasn't guiding us, but like a good host he showed us as much of the good stuff as he could in the time we had: not only the big, luxurious pools with parking-lot–sized turnouts that we could have found on our own, but the inside dope on runs that looked good but seldom if ever held fish (who knew why?), as well as froggy-looking tubs that could be inexplicably productive.

I especially remember one such slot right along the riprap from the canyon road. When Jeff showed it to me, it looked too slow, too deep and otherwise all wrong for steelhead. But I dutifully fished it, and once I figured out the cast, some trick of hydrology made the fly swim perfectly with no effort at all on my part. I worked this water slowly and carefully and pretty soon I was expecting a tug on every cast. It didn't happen, but once you feel a fish welling up, the feeling doesn't go away, even after it's been proved wrong. This was a run that would eventually give up a steelhead if you gave it the time it deserved, even if all I got that time was a nicely waking fly.

After I'd fished out the run and was walking back to our truck along the road, I saw a woman coming toward me on the shoulder. The first thing I noticed was that this was an attractive young woman in waders (a real weakness of mine). The second thing I noticed was that she looked seriously pissed off.

When we got close enough, she asked, in an accusing tone, "Are you guys shooting a movie?"

"Are we what?"

"Shooting a movie! I saw your truck!"

It took me a minute to piece this together. Doug is part owner of a small company that distributes fly-fishing movies, and we'd driven out from Colorado in the crew cab pickup that serves as the company car. In the back window of that truck, plain as day, was a sticker that reads FLYFISHINGFILMTOUR.COM. That's when the light went on. The thought of your home water starring in a movie that's shown to thousands of fly casters, all desperate for the next hot spot, is enough to strike first fear and then righteous anger in the heart of any fisherman.

I sputtered out an explanation to the effect that Doug's company just distributes films, they don't make them, and that we were just fishing, and that anyway I was just a friend along for the ride and had nothing whatsoever to do with show business. I added that if she wanted to know more she'd have to talk to Doug himself. I know that last part was cowardly, but I've had an instinctive fear of angry women ever since first grade, when I was regularly scolded by females who outweighed me by a hundred pounds.

I must have seemed craven enough to take the wind out of her sails because all she could think to say was, "Well, you ought'a cover up that sticker before someone slashes your tires!"

As I walked back to the truck, I idly wondered if she'd been about to slash our tires when she saw me walking down the road, and the thought of an angry woman with a knife made my knees go all wobbly.

By this time we'd moved out of Jeff and Jan's house and into a room closer to the river in the small town of Klickitat. Our new digs were half a block from the Canyon Market with its good breakfast burritos and fresh coffee, and a hundred feet from the Town Pool. This is where high school kids fish for steelhead before class and where they've claimed the place as their own by tagging a cliff with spray paint. So when I went outside early the next morning, I wasn't surprised to see a kid walking up the street wearing Leon Trotsky-style wire-rimmed glasses, a faded BORN TO BE BAD T-shirt and carrying a spinning rod and a hatchery steelhead. I gave him a wave. He raised his rod tip slightly in response, acknowledging the compliment while remaining aloof.

A kid walking home with a fish is a nostalgic item for me anyway, and since we'd all killed some hatchery fish ourselves recently, there was a heightened sense of companionship. Hatchery steelhead are inferior in every way to wild fish and in a perfect world they wouldn't exist. On the other hand, they're good to eat, legal to keep and this was a year into the worst recession since the 1930s, so a good free meal was no small thing. Whenever one of us landed a steelhead with a clipped adipose fin—the universal mark of hatchery origin—someone would be there to say, "If you don't want it, I'll take it."

If the truth were known, none of us was exactly on top of things in the area of personal finances (never mind the particulars, which are nobody's business), but we were fishing, so we didn't dwell on it. Still, I couldn't help recalling the endless stories about the Great Depression I heard as a kid—all those geezers proudly saying, "We didn't have a pot to piss in, but we worked hard, made our own fun and we never went hungry."

I know there are assistance programs for people who are down on their luck, but I also know from experience that they often come at too high a price in self-respect. Once, back in the late 1960s, I went on food stamps for a month out of what I thought was necessity. The experience was so demeaning that I'd have felt better about myself if I'd just held up a gas station for grocery money. With that in mind, I found it nearly as satisfying to kill a hatchery steelhead that would be someone's dinner as to release a wild one. In virtually every case, wild steelhead are too rare and precious to be eaten, but it's the occasional meal of a hatchery fish that keeps the sport from becoming too cerebral.

Just the day before, a local fisherman and his dog had arrived at the river in a pickup that seemed to be burning more oil than gas and had stepped in below me as I fished down a run. I naturally bristled for all the good it did. A spey caster's personal space is about the same as that of a sow grizzly with cubs, although we don't enforce it with anywhere near the same authority. But then later on we bumped into each other and got to talking. The guy explained—a little sheepishly—that he'd been in town looking for work with no luck and thought he'd at least try for a fish dinner before he came home to his wife empty-handed again. That struck me as a passable excuse even in less troubled economic times. I also met his yellow Lab, who turned out to be a slightly dim-witted but lovable goofball, and decided I couldn't stay mad at a guy who owned a happy dog and honestly needed a fish for supper.

Later that same day I was working down a long pool known poetically as "Number Four," where we'd caught a couple of fish over the last few days. By then I was in the usual steelheader's trance, thinking about how straight each cast laid out, the angle of the fly to the current, the speed of the swing and so on, but also somehow thinking of nothing much at all.

I'd made one pass through the pool with a size 4 Undertaker—a handsome fly I've always loved if only for the name—and when I didn't move anything, I started another pass with a smaller Steelhead Muddler. Right at the head of a riffly tub that we'd come to know as the sweet spot, I got a boil at the fly and a little tap. I fished out the cast in case the fish wanted to follow the fly and hit it again, but no dice.

I showed him the Muddler again, but got no apparent reaction, so I stripped in and changed to a small, dark comeback fly that I'd copied from a pattern of Scott's. (I won't describe it in case it's a secret.) The fish hit on the first swing with the kind of angry grab you hope for and came completely out of the water. Jeff saw it from a distance and later guessed it would have gone ten pounds. I thought more like twelve.

The fish stayed in the pool through several good runs and a few more jumps and then came off just as I was beaching it. He threw the hook in six inches of water and was gone so fast I didn't even have time to try to tackle him.

By this time Jeff, Doug and Vince had wandered over to watch the show, and when the hook came loose, we all shared a moment of silence. They understood that you beat yourself up over a lost steelhead as if you'd just gambled away the mortgage payment in a poker game, so they said the only things you *can* say by way of consolation: that this was clearly a wild fish that I'd have released anyway, so hooking it was what counted, while landing it would have just been a formality. That was bullshit, of course, but it was meant kindly.

.

19

SMALLIES

I was northbound on U.S. Highway 63 in western Wisconsin, nearing the end of the long drive from Colorado in a peculiar state of mind. If you've never experienced one, it's impossible to describe the quality of road trance these solitary drives can induce. Suffice it to say that after thinking things over for the last eleven hundred miles, I'd arrived at the inescapable conclusion that at the right distance and in a certain light, a mature cottonwood tree looks like an enormous head of broccoli.

Highway 63 is one of those rural two-lane blacktops that are in no particular hurry. It takes its own sweet time meandering past farms and lakes at an average speed limit of forty-five miles an hour—which seemed like walking speed after the interstate—and then slowing abruptly to twenty-five as it becomes the main street of one small town after another. At this point I was in no hurry either. Up till then it had all been about making time, and through Nebraska and Iowa I'd enjoyed the symmetry of going eighty miles an hour on Interstate 80. But by then I was within two hours or so of Hayward, where I'd meet my friends Wendy Williamson and Larry Mann, who run the only fly shop in town. It was two o'clock in the afternoon and we wouldn't be fishing until tomorrow, so I had all the time in the world to drift into town, pick up a fishing license and move into the empty apartment above the shop that they were letting me use. I wouldn't have to wait for them to come back from their respective guide trips to get in. This being northern Wisconsin, the apartment would either be unlocked or the key would be under the mat.

I spent part of my youth around here—next door in Minnesota, actually—but for the purpose of nostalgia I claim this entire region as my home ground, more or less from the Dakotas east to Lake Michigan. My family moved around when I was young, so I lived in other places as a kid, but those years in the upper Midwest were what they'd now call pivotal. The place was a paradise for the kind of sportsman I aspired to be, and I was finally old enough to paddle a canoe, run an outboard, and fish and hunt without undue supervision. I'd also long since figured out that girls were more than just boys who dressed funny, and I was then on the verge of working out what a guy might actually do about that, given sufficient courage. In other words, I was just beginning to glimpse the field of adult possibilities that I haven't yet exhausted after almost fifty years.

Of course, things have changed since then—including me—but I still feel oddly at home here as you do in a place where you no longer belong but did once. I've never dared to go back to the lakes I fished as a kid for obvious reasons, but I've been back to the general area several times, and aside from cellphones, video rentals and the odd sign advertising AWESOME YOGA MATS, things seem pretty much as I remember them. The countryside is still a patchwork of farms, lakes, rivers and woods; many small towns still have statues of walleyes instead of war heroes in the park; cheese curds—the by-product left over when actual cheese is made—are still inexplicably considered a delicacy and waitresses still call you "Hon."

So with time on my hands I stopped for lunch at a roadhouse straight out of my idyllic youth, with deer and fish mounts on the walls and Formica booths with cracked plastic seats patched with duct tape. I ordered the regulation hot pork sandwich on white bread with a pound of mashed potatoes on the side (no vegetables), the whole thing slathered with industrial-strength brown gravy. The waitress who delivered this feast was a cheerful three-hundred-pounder, in case there was any doubt about the dangers inherent in a steady diet of midwestern comfort food.

The next morning Wendy and I floated a stretch of the Chippewa River. It was a warm, sunny June day after a week of steady rain, so we dawdled more than we normally would in the morning to let the water warm up. On the drive to the river, the woods looked lush and steamy and there were fresh puddles on the shoulder.

This spell of soggy weather had gone on intermittently for weeks by then and was shaping up not as an isolated event, but as a definitive break in the drought that had kept the rivers worrisomely skinny for the last several years. It's an article of faith in the Midwest that when rain spoils a picnic, "at least we need the moisture," but in this case it was God's own truth.

The Chippewa was now bank-full and Wendy's sense of relief had settled into a kind of suppressed giddiness. Fluctuations in the weather used to be just that, but now, with everyone looking over their shoulders at global climate change, there's the fear that any extreme could become the new normal. And when you guide fishermen for a living, the thought of your rivers drying up is the stuff of nightmares. So Wendy kept pointing out sunken gravel bars that had been bone-dry last year and submerged rocks that used to be ten feet up the bank. She really wanted me to visualize it and I *did* remember walking the boat over some bony spots on this river a few years before, but in the end I was just another tourist whose curse is never to fully comprehend the backstory.

We caught nice-sized smallmouth bass on top water bugs at what I thought was a fairly good clip. There'd be fifteen minutes of fruitless casting followed by a fishy bank where I'd get five hits and hook and land two or three fat bass. Wendy said the fishing was slow, but then guides endure so many clients who expect nonstop thrills that they sometimes lose sight of reality. In fact, this was perfectly good fishing for someone who still believes—in spite of a lifetime's worth of evidence to the contrary—that catching fish is pretty unlikely. Most of the fishermen I know fully expect to land something when they head out in the morning, but for some reason I'm still as skeptical of the whole business as I was at age five when I first lowered a baited hook out of sight over the gunnel of a rowboat. I was the kind of kid who was easily fooled and some mean older boys had already sent me on a snipe hunt, so I thought this could be yet another practical joke.

The bass were scattered that day, as they tend to be in a river that's recently risen several feet. You can get technical about what this means to both fish and fishermen, but it comes down to bare statistics: You've got the same number of bass as before, now spread out in twice as much water and as puzzled as you'd be if your neighborhood suddenly doubled in size.

Of course, when bass get flummoxed, they hunker down in the thickest cover to wait things out, so the best cast was one that tucked the bug in so tight that its rubber legs were hugging a rock or log. The fish wouldn't move far for a fly, but when it was right where they wanted it, you'd get those quick, precise takes that are unlike those of any other game fish.

Smallies have the air about them of being all business. They're compact, chunky and muscular; greenish-bronze-colored overall with broken brownish olive vertical bars to break up their silhouettes. They're so beautifully camouflaged that sometimes it's hard to see one in clear water even when it's within a leader's length of the boat. In the hand they feel hard, cool, slick and vaguely grainy. Every few years some fishing industry wonk declares that smallmouth bass are poised to become "the next trout" in some bottom-line marketing sense, but so far they've persisted in being just what they are. If a brook trout comes off as a delicate creature on its way to a party, a smallmouth bass is a guy in coveralls clocking in at work.

I bore down and made some accurate casts, some of which drew strikes. Every once in a while, Wendy would quietly say "Nice," the single word that, coming from a guide, makes a fly caster's heart soar. Of course, other casts fell far short of accurate, as usual, leaving me to wonder what the hell just happened. When you make a near-perfect cast, or even two or three real nice ones in a row, you naturally wonder why they can't all be that good because apparently you have it in you. Likewise, when you occasionally say just the right thing, you wonder why you say the wrong thing so often.

The next day the rain was back, and Larry and I floated the Namekagon in a steady, daylong downpour. Foul weather adds an emotional dimension to the boondocks, and although the river was within sight and sound of a state highway in places, it looked as remotely beautiful and deserted as a tributary of the Amazon. We had it all to ourselves. No one else was dumb enough to be out in a boat in the pouring rain.

We caught bass at a leisurely pace through the morning,

alternating between Larry's current favorite bug, the Umpqua Swimming Baitfish, and some fabulous bass bugs that had been sent to me out of the blue by a Frenchman named Jacques Bordenave, who had read and liked some of my books. These were some of the most flawlessly tied deer-hair bugs I've ever seen. Jacques had designed them brilliantly along the lines of a Whitlock Diving Frog, only more elaborately colored—"for the pleasure of the eyes," he said—and with wider, flatter bodies that made them dive deeper and wiggle more seductively. The fish liked them and so did the half-dozen bass fishermen I showed them to. They all wanted to know where they could buy some, and I enjoyed putting on airs by saying that they were tied for me privately in France and were unavailable commercially.

It must have been midafternoon when the fishing shut off completely. The water temperature had been cool to begin with and according to Larry's digital stream thermometer, the rain had been chilling the river at the rate of about a degree per hour. Bass are all about water temperature, and when it approaches and then passes their lower avoidance level, the jig is up, simple as that. We anchored out for lunch and sat with our backs to the wind, hunched over to make dry spots just big enough to keep our sandwiches from getting soggy. At this point someone is required to say, "You know, there are people who wouldn't think this is fun."

I can't recall if I kept casting as we rowed out, or just watched the river go by. I know there were several miles to go to the takeout, but in my memory, the day ended while we were still hunched over our ham sandwiches. My notes don't help. All I wrote in my trip log that night was "Tuesday it rained." What else can you say?

Wednesday was still raw and gray, but the rain had petered off to intermittent, gusty squalls. There were periods of as much as half an hour when you could lower the hood on your rain jacket. This increases your peripheral vision and relieves the claustrophobic sense that you're casting from inside a culvert.

Larry took me to a stretch of the West Fork of the Chippewa that he hadn't been able to fish for several years. The river here flows through flat country with a current so imperceptible it gives the impression of being a long, skinny lake. But to get in there you have to negotiate a quarter mile or so of rocks and riffle below the put-in that, until recently, hadn't had enough water to float a drift boat.

Larry said we might get a musky in here and the place had that look to it. Dense mats of wild rice, bulrushes, cattails and arrowroot bordered the slow channel. The water was clear but stained the color of strong orange pekoe tea from all the rain percolating through a forest floor made of pine duff and dead leaves, giving everything under the surface a metallic reddish cast. It was the perfect place for a big ambush predator with the unlikely combination of glacial patience and a short fuse.

Muskies are a fact of life in these rivers; so smart bass fishers tie their flies onto fifty-pound fluorocarbon shock tippets to avoid losing too many expensive deer-hair bugs. Some traditional musky lures can be a foot long, but early in the season muskies eat the same frogs, mice, crawdads and small baitfish that bass do. On previous trips I'd caught a few muskies by mistake while bass fishing, and at other times I'd targeted them specifically—with equal results and using the same flies. Whether I expected them or not, they were among the nastiest things I'd ever hooked on a fly rod. Of course, I mean "nasty" in the best possible sense.

Larry opened one of his briefcase-sized plastic fly boxes and handed me a large gray and white swimming baitfish pattern with an orange band around its middle. It didn't look like any living thing I'd ever seen, but it looked good and I obediently tied it on. There's some intuition to fly selection and on his home water I trust Larry's more than mine.

In a deep spot in that short stretch of fast water, I hooked a small bass off the bank and missed a musky I didn't see but that Larry said wasn't that big. It was a beginner's mistake. With the fly still in the water, I'd glanced up to look for the next spot at the same moment that I began the strip for my back cast. The fish naturally chose that instant to nip at the fly. There are a thousand things to know about muskies, but only two that are crucial. One is that if a musky follows your fly and you stop or even slow the retrieve, he'll lose interest and go away. The other is that he's fearless and will often follow the fly right to the boat, so you should never, ever take your eyes off it.

I picked up a few more small bass that day, but mostly it was the long, steady slog of musky fishing, where it can be hours if not days between strikes. Once an ominous bulge followed my fly for a few feet off a bank, but nothing came of it. Later, on what had become just another one of hundreds of casts, there was a sudden, violent rush of water and a splash that resembled an anvil dropping in the water. Out of shock and awe, I set up too soon and ripped the fly away before the big musky could grab it.

Larry put on a professorial voice and said, "In my role as guide, I'd now normally say that you should wait till you feel the weight of the fish before you set the hook, but there's nothing I can do about fifty years' worth of ingrained reflex." In other words, you fucked it up, but then you already know that.

On the morning of what would have been my last day of fishing, I was awakened before dawn by what sounded like a street sweeper going by outside the window. But it didn't go by, and when I got up to look, it turned out to be the roar of pounding rain punctuated by flashes of lightning. When I heard Larry come in to open the shop, I went downstairs and we stood with cups of coffee looking out at a frog strangler that all but obscured the ice-cream shop across the street. It would have gone without saying, but after a clap of thunder that rattled the windows, Larry said, "I don't know about you, but I'm not going fishing today."

The day before, Wendy and I had done a float on the beautiful

Flambeau River, where I'd caught just the right number of bass—enough to lose count, but not so many as to ruin the sightseeing—including one late in the day that was as close to perfect as they get. He wasn't all that big, but he had nosed into a narrow divot in the bank like a car parked in a garage. My cast put the deer-hair body of the fly in the water with its tail lying on the grassy bank and the fish all but crawled up on dry land to eat it. Wendy said, "That guy was holding a little tight." That may or may not have been the last fish of the trip, but it's the last one I remember.

Back at the fly shop, two customers in full rain gear came in after shaking off like wet dogs on the front steps. They were dressed for fishing and bought some flies, but instead of bustling back out again, they joined Larry and me as we stared blankly out at the downpour. I was thinking about my long drive home, which would take the better part of two days. Larry might have been thinking about the clients he had booked over the coming weekend, when even if the rain stopped, the rivers would be too cold for bass. He'd have been weighing a few days of poor fishing against the enduring condition of the rivers and taking the long view.

The customers had been all bluster and determination when they came in but now seemed on the verge of changing their minds. All four of us just stood there for what seemed like the longest time.

20

MARCH

There can be dead spells in the sporting life. Droughts. Bugaboos. Runs of bad luck. Sometimes they seem to build from an innocent catastrophe that, in hindsight, looks like a precipitating event. For instance, I've just finished writing a book and am getting ready for a late winter steelhead trip to the West Coast. I'm a little burned out and this is just what I need: a long stretch of time away from the desk stepping and casting with a spey rod. This isn't mindless fishing as some claim (a friend who says it could be done just as well by a zombie is wrong), but it's true that it doesn't demand a lot of deep thinking.

But then the trip is abruptly canceled. One partner has unexpected work conflicts and he owns the company, so can't pawn them off. The other partner and I decide to go without him, but then he tries to move a large safe by himself and detaches a tendon in his left bicep. He says he could hear it break as well as feel it. I imagine it sounding like a rubber band snapping inside a wet plastic bag. This after I ask if he needs help and he says, "Naw, I got it."

I forgive him for wrecking the fishing trip the way you forgive a puppy that eats the couch because he doesn't know he shouldn't. This is a big guy who not only doesn't know his own strength but is also unclear about his limitations. Once while four-wheeling, I watched him jump out of the truck and try to move a Volkswagen-sized boulder that was blocking the road. It would have taken a backhoe to so much as budge this thing, even if it hadn't been attached by the roots to the entire span of the northern Rockies, but he was genuinely surprised that he couldn't just roll it out of the way.

He has an operation to reattach the tendon and for the next six weeks can't even use that arm to lift a coffee cup, let alone cast a spey rod. I think about going on the trip by myself but don't have the heart for it. The biggest steelhead can come in late winter, but they come so seldom they can begin to seem nonexistent, and the weather is always grim. I try to picture the long fishless hours alone for day after day in the usual cold rain. It's a romantic image, but it keeps going out of focus. I enjoy fishing by myself, but there are some sports—and winter steelheading is one of them—where you need a partner to help you cowboy up. Otherwise you can spend too much time in warm, dry cafés and motel rooms wondering why you drove twelve hundred miles when you could do this at home.

A canceled fishing trip creates a specific vacuum that can't be filled with just any old thing, so I make several day trips to the famous tailwater a two-hour drive to the south. Fishing reports from the fly shop down there are generically favorable but lack the enthusiasm you hope for. On the other hand, a guide I know says he's whacking them pretty good down around Long Scraggy some days. But those apparently aren't the days I'm there. On my best afternoon I manage to land two small, confused-looking trout. One is hooked fairly in the mouth on a miniature Glo Bug pattern known as a Nuclear Egg; the other is foul-hooked under a pectoral fin. I tell myself he went for my size 22 midge pupa and missed, but know in my heart that he'd been minding his own business when I inadvertently snagged him.

The small tailwater closer to home has stayed locked up with ice through the canyon longer than usual. It's been a colder and wetter winter than normal. Not by a lot—just a few degrees and a few inches—but global climate change has taught us that it doesn't take much to make a big difference. Even friends who aren't old and cranky have been complaining about the hard winter.

Still, if you're a fly fisherman in the Colorado Rockies, you push spring hard knowing how short it will be and how early the window can open. Even after forty-one years here, I can't get used to hearing my first meadowlark during a snowstorm or seeing the freestone rivers get wide, deep and brown just as the cottonwoods begin to leaf out. By the time it's what most would think of as fishing weather, with green grass, flowers and birds singing at dawn, the rivers are in full runoff and it's time to pack your stuff and blow town in search of clear water.

Meanwhile, up in the canyon, I'm reduced to teetering out on the shelf ice to dredge nymphs in the occasional slot of open water. I manage to hook a few trout, but I keep wondering what I'll do if the ice breaks loose with me standing on it. I've felt thirty-four-degree water go down my waders before and that vivid memory makes it hard to concentrate. And there's the story of the fisherman who drowned when he was knocked down and pushed under by a floating ice sheet. That was on a different river, bit still . . . Then the Highway Department closes the canyon road to work on the bridges, and that's that for a while. It's almost a relief.

I check out a stream at a lower elevation that's recently been stocked with a kind of hybrid rainbow that's supposed to be resistant to whirling disease. I've been wondering if this is a good idea. The wild browns in there have a natural immunity and seem to have held up fairly well against this insidious foreign parasite, and although there aren't a lot of them, I suspect there are as many as the stream's modest biomass can support. Still, I'm curious. I fish a small brown fly I think they'll take as a pellet of Trout Chow. The fish are cute little baby rainbows with parr marks and they're all a uniform four inches long. Most can't get a size 20 fly sideways in their little mouths, and when one does, the trick is to set the hook without flipping him over your shoulder. I spot a few larger browns, but the eager babies always beat them to the fly.

This gets old quickly. On the walk back to the truck, I flush a blue heron that's so full of these little stockers he can barely get airborne.

I drive over to the West Slope to check out another small tailwater, crossing a 13,000-foot pass with icy, fifteen-mile-an-hour switchbacks near the top. The snow up there would be chest-deep on an elk if the elk hadn't all wisely migrated to lower altitudes to wait out winter. At that altitude it's well below freezing, the sky is a cloudless, robin's-egg blue and the snow is so bright I can hardly look at it even through sunglasses. I'm the only vehicle up there that doesn't have skis strapped to the roof.

On the west side of the pass, I drive through one of those soulless ski towns with a solid business plan but no character or history. I pass up a Starbucks and drive on into the ranch country along the upper Colorado River. In a blue-collar café down there, I get a cup of coffee that doesn't cost seven dollars, doesn't come with whipped cream and sprinkles, and isn't served by a blond girl named Tiffany.

I posthole to the river through eighteen inches of wet snow that make the level mile feel more like six miles uphill, envying the person who went in ahead of me leaving cross-country ski tracks. The river itself is a pretty little thing sparsely bordered in cottonwood and juniper, meandering through its shallow valley between steep snowbanks like something out of Currier & Ives. I don't carry a stream thermometer, but a finger stuck in the river begins to sting in four seconds, which puts the water temperature in the mid-thirties. I'm hoping for a midge hatch, but there are no telltale flies in the air and no rises or boils on the water. So I put together the standard Colorado winter rig—two small nymphs, a twist of weight and a chartreuse Thingamabobber—and go to work.

I run into four other fishermen that day. One says he landed two brown trout early and then nothing. The other three say they haven't had a touch or even seen a fish all day. I say, "Yeah, me too."

On the walk back to the pickup, I cross the tracks of a large elk herd that had passed through the previous night. There must have been close to a hundred animals. A wide swath of snow looks like it was rototilled and sprinkled with small black turds. I had a granola bar and half a bottle of water for lunch, but that was hours ago and I've slogged through a lot of deep snow since then. Suddenly, I'm ravenous for a medium-rare elk burger smothered in A.1. steak sauce. There's still fifteen pounds of elk burger left from last fall's hunt, but it's three hours away and frozen solid, so I'll have to settle for a Big Mac.

This isn't the worst slump I've ever had. This is just the slack that comes with marginal conditions and seasonal impatience. There's something to be said for seeing your home water in all its moods instead of just when it's at its best—it's the difference between being a tourist and a resident—but the old insecurities kick in anyway. Is the fishing really this slow, or am I just going through the motions without benefit of inspiration? Should I keep plugging away, or pack it in and do something else entirely, like cleaning out the garage? I assume this will pass because it always has before, but for the time being it seems permanent.

Of course, I pride myself on being a fisherman who's not especially interested in competition—and not just because I usually lose. But then I'm also at large in the twenty-first century when it's hard to find a fishing magazine that doesn't have the words "catch more" and "bigger" emblazoned on the cover. So where my father would have shrugged and said the fish aren't bitin', I now have to suspect that I'm not deploying the proper technology. I tell myself it's only fishing and my confidence shouldn't be so fragile.

I call a contact out West to see how the steelheading has been. "Kind of slow," he says, "and it's been raining, but I've had a few hatchery fish and one wild hen about ten pounds. I'm hoping it'll pick up."

I stop in to see my injured friend. He's making progress, but he's still in a cast, more than a little bored and not too happy about being sidelined from the fishing. I tell him he hasn't been missing much. He appreciates the sentiment and feels a little better, but, like any fisherman, he secretly thinks that if he'd been there he'd have caught fish. He may be right.

The next day I stop to see a boatbuilder friend who tells me the ice up in the canyon has cleared, midges are hatching and the road opened two days ago. There are flagmen and construction delays, but at least you can drive down there now. The guy has been too busy making boats to go fishing himself, but he heard this firsthand through his extensive grapevine, so it's reliable.

Driving to the river the next morning, I remember a reviewer of sporting books saying you can work so hard at being a trout bum that your fishing becomes an example of the Puritan ethic you set out to escape in the first place. Well, maybe, but most fishermen are single-minded enough to be immune to criticism. We rarely question what we're doing, only how we're doing it. I remind myself of a decades-old vow to disregard the opinions of reviewers whenever I feel like it.

Two miles down the canyon I'm stopped by a flagman in front of the still-closed-for-the-season Whispering Pine Motel. I sit there long enough to think about turning off the engine to save gas, but just as I'm reaching for the key, he lets me through. I pull off at a good pool a hundred yards downstream of the roadwork to take a look at the water. There are patches of snow in the canyon and some old, dirty ice along the banks, but the river is completely open. It's still at a low winter flow, so the long tail of the pool is glassy and I can clearly see trout rising.

I'm more excited than usual, but I make a point of rigging up slowly and methodically, cinching the boots a little too tight to allow for the laces to stretch when they get wet; stringing the rod with the fly line bent double so if I drop it, it will catch in a guide and not all snake out on the ground; stretching the memory coils out of the leader and checking it for wind knots. All the same things and always in the same order in the belief that if I get the beginning right, the part that comes next might go more smoothly.

The trout are rising to a steady hatch of midges, so I tie on a local favorite midge pattern—size 22, black—and start in the slack water in the tail of the pool. This is a cloudy but bright morning with the kind of diffuse light that at one angle makes water so transparent it's as if it isn't even there and at another turns the river to a sheet of pewter. In the smooth tail of the pool where I can see them clearly, I hook two small browns at the end of long, slow drifts and spook another fish I didn't see with one of my casts. Several other trout inspect the fly but aren't convinced. I hang an unweighted midge pupa off the dry fly on an eighteen-inch dropper, squeeze it wet and catch one of the fish that didn't like the floating fly.

Then I work a few casts out into the faster current where I can see rises but can't spot the fish. I miss one strike and then hook a bigger rainbow. He takes a little line and comes in stubbornly. He's not all that much longer than the browns I've already landed, but he's muscular and has a deep, hard belly, a thickly spotted deep green back and a brilliant reddish-orange lateral stripe. This river had a slump of its own years ago after a terrible flash flood, but it's come back nicely and now has a reputation for real pretty trout and lots of them. They're wild catch-and-release fish and no pushovers, but they're feeding heavily now, so they're at a disadvantage. Robert Traver once said, "Funny thing, I become a hell of a good fisherman when the trout decide to commit suicide."

My next strike is a heavier fish. It's a longer cast up into bumpy, chromy water where I can't see the little fly, so I slap the water to see where it lands and then follow the drift. When I see a dark snout come up where I think the fly should be, I wait the exact half second it takes for the fish to take and turn and then set just hard enough to break the 7x tippet. I try to think of a way that this isn't my fault, but can't come up with anything.

I rerig with another dry fly and catch five or six more trout before the hatch goes off. The last one takes a while. He's lying in the soft current along the far bank picking off strays, and even after I've worked out the drift, he doesn't like the fly I'm using. I switch to a fly I copied from a Roy Palm pattern: just a few wraps of black thread on a size 22 hook with one turn of dun-colored soft hackle at the head. Greased lightly with fly floatant, it lies flush and messy on the surface like a crippled or stillborn midge fly. The fish picks it up on the first good drift and runs downstream, where I net him in the tail of the pool. It's another chunky, handsome rainbow.

And that's the end of it. I think about rigging up some nymphs and working the deep water, but I don't really need any more fish and feel like quitting on a high note. At this point I begin to hear the backup horn on a road grader upstream. It's probably been there all along, but this is the first time in almost three hours that I've noticed it.

At the head of the canyon I drive past the shortcut over to the road home and go on into town. I stop for a cup of coffee to go and then stroll down the block to say hello to Steve at the fly shop. I'm hoping he'll ask how I did this morning.

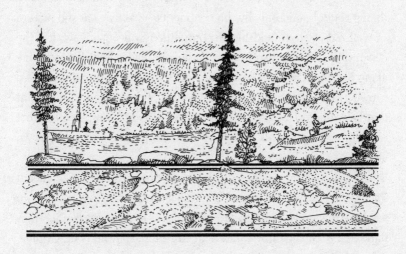

21

CHINOOKS

The first Chinook salmon I caught here was a twenty-five-pound buck. He made several long runs and spent quite a while bulldogging before I got him in the shallows where I could slip out of the boat onto a firm bottom to land him. A moment comes while playing a big fish when things begin to turn in your favor, but even then there's only one way it can go right and dozens of ways it can go wrong, all of which will be your fault. So when he was finally in the net, I felt more relief than triumph.

After a number of years at sea in what Russell Chatham called "a dining room bound only by the continents," this fish was the picture of well-fed strength and health, but although he may have left the ocean only a day or two before, he already had a faint flush of pink along his flanks and a pale bronze cast on the back reminiscent of a brown trout. That meant his metabolism had changed to the point that he would no longer feed, and after I released him, he'd live first off his fat and then his muscle as he continued upstream to spawn and die.

Anyone who's caught and released one of these magnificent Pacific salmon should probably go up into the headwaters later to see how this ends. There will be your fish—or one just like it—now darkened to the color of a waterlogged stump, spawned out, gasping, exhausted, fining weakly in the current as he quietly falls apart. You wonder if he had any inkling of this when he swam out of the ocean shiny as a chrome bumper and horny as a billy goat. No telling. I've looked into the eyes of caught salmon before and what I've seen is not something I recognized as comprehension.

The estuary Rob Russell and I were fishing ran smack through one of those small coastal towns that have shaped their outlines and character around the mouths of rivers. In places, the bank above the high-water mark was lined with cottages, and although some were newer than others, they all shared the graying driftwood look of houses near an ocean. A few were built so low to the water it seemed like a high runoff or a good tidal surge would swamp them. In an unexpected adult moment, I caught myself wondering about the availability of flood insurance. I lived on the water myself for twenty-one years and know that to have a river for a neighbor is to have a streak of wildness in your backyard. It's beautiful and familiar, but also as unpredictably dangerous as a half-tame mountain lion.

It's tempting to say that everyone who lived there not only fished, but also went about it with some expectation of success. I'm sure that's not strictly true (all towns have their misfits), but on any given day it seemed as though every able-bodied adult was out in a boat or lined up casting from the bank at the Bridge Pool. Most were fishing bait and many wore rubber gloves to protect their hands from the caustic brine commercial salmon eggs come packaged in. In one backyard a middle-aged couple was casting from the lawn while a barbeque grill smoldered on the porch and the family cat lounged nearby waiting for a fresh salmon. Even in town, everyone was dressed in rubber boots and rain slickers for the drizzly October weather and could have at least passed as a fisherman.

The Chinook run was on and the estuary was bustling with fishing boats. It looked like the kind of event that might have been dreamed up by the Chamber of Commerce. The only thing missing was a banner across Main Street reading GOOD OL' SALMON DAZE! But as festive as it looked from a distance, the atmosphere on the water was sometimes tense as boats angled for position at the known honey holes. The boundaries of personal space were in question and the occasional cold shoulders, territorial stares and unreturned greetings were hard to miss, but there was also the tacit acknowledgment that if you were too polite or timid, you'd never get a spot to fish.

Fly fishermen don't always fit seamlessly into this scene. Bait is the gold standard here, and some may still remember when it was assumed that you couldn't catch Chinooks on a fly—the same thing they once said about permit. That's long since been proved wrong, but the idea that a fly rod isn't appropriate tackle for Chinooks hasn't entirely died out.

For one thing, fly fishers are still referred to by some as "snaggers," and in fact, foul-hooking can be a problem if you fish a sinking line through pods of salmon with the traditional down-and-across swing. So many have taken to anchoring fore and aft at right angles to the current, casting steeply downstream and fishing a narrow swing and retrieve. But then that upsets the natural order of boats anchored parallel to the current and can leave the impression that you're covering more water than you deserve.

Fly fishers are also said to let their fish run too far. That would normally be your own business, but etiquette at least suggests that when a hooked fish runs in your direction you should raise your anchor to avoid fouling the line. When a salmon is attached to a fly rod, some still weigh anchor and move as a matter of course, others do it grudgingly—complete with theatrical eye-rolling—and still others pointedly stay put believing that if you'd just fish the way you're supposed to, you could winch that sucker in without inconveniencing your neighbors. These are the people who think those of us who fish for Chinooks with a fly rod are out to prove something—which of course we are.

Rob negotiates all this deftly. For one thing, his credentials as a local fisherman are impeccable. He's fished here for years and he guided both bait and fly fishermen for a decade, so he's known to some of these guys personally and to others by reputation. For another, he shoulders his way in with the aggressive neighborliness of a door-to-door salesman, cheerfully refusing to take no for an answer.

This kind of fishing revolves around the tides. There are no sure things, but as a rule of thumb, dark salmon bite best on a falling and low tide while bright fish bite on the rising tide they came in on from the sea—when they bite at all. Fish roll off and on throughout the day, but there's often more activity on a high tide as fresh salmon jostle around in the holding water with the fish that are already there. Maybe they bite as a way of establishing territory, or out of habit, or nervousness, or curiosity. Some takes seem to be no more than quizzical nudges and can turn out to be either a twenty-pound salmon or a four-inch sculpin known as a "pogie." Other hits seem downright murderous.

Everyone has a working theory about when, why and how salmon bite—factoring in things like river flow, wind direction, rainfall, cloud cover, barometric pressure and such—while at the same time allowing that migratory fish often respond to signals that mere humans can't detect or understand. In the end, these estimations are largely psychological devices designed to give shape to your enthusiasm even as real life does its best to intrude. Rob said he once e-mailed a friend telling him when to be there to catch the tide. The friend e-mailed back, "I'll meet you at the boat ramp as soon as I get through with marriage counseling."

But theories or not, the tactics are invariably the same: locate a spot where salmon congregate and keep a hook in the water. If you were unfamiliar with the estuary, the most dependable holding water would be easy to find. It's where all the boats are anchored.

Even if you've seen it before, this business of tides takes some getting used to. On a low tide the current runs downstream to the sea and it's fresh water. As the tide turns, the current slows, stalls and then begins to flow in the opposite direction. If you were to taste the water then, it would be brackish or salty and as you stare distractedly at your rod tip held close to the water, a jellyfish might swim by. The word "estuary" is defined either as a place where a river meets the sea or where the sea meets a river, but the exact point where that happens changes from minute to minute. This is disorienting to those of us from the Colorado Rockies, where, whatever else happens, water always flows downhill.

And there are the seals. They sometimes come far upriver following the salmon and reveal themselves with wakes reminiscent of nuclear submarines or when they pop their heads above the surface to take a breath and look around. Some say they put off the fishing and others say they just reveal the presence of salmon. I don't have a firm opinion, but several times I saw seals blast through a pod of salmon, only to have the fish start rolling again ten minutes later. The first time I saw a seal in a salmon river was just upstream from Chiginagak Bay on the Alaska Peninsula. I mistook the bobbing black head for a Labrador retriever and asked the guy next to me, "Whose dog is that?"

Salmon fishing would bore the pants off a normal American with an attention span conditioned by television. Of course, there's the initial strategy of deciding on your spot and the little drama of getting it. To beat the rush, perhaps you settle on known prime water and show up an hour early for the tide. That can work, but it's not an original idea and there might well be five boats ahead of you that showed up even earlier. So maybe you crowd in around the edges or, if you're with someone like Rob who knows the estuary better than most, you try an obscure tub that's small, won't hold a lot of salmon and is productive only under certain conditions of time, tide and weather, but that you'll have to yourself.

Then you choose a sink tip to fit the depth and current speed and decide on a fly. If you've recently caught a fish or had a take on something, you stick with it. Otherwise you open the yellow plastic boat box and gaze at the rows of mostly medium-sized, predominantly orange or pink long-tailed Comet variations. If a nonangler were to ask how you make your decision, you wouldn't know what to say, but intuition shouldn't be discounted. I've seen lots of sea-run fish caught on flies a fisherman held up and said, "Damn it, I just like the looks of this."

Finally you cast either straight downstream or at a narrow angle to the current and don't do much else. Now and then, you'll break things up with a fast or slow halting retrieve, but the majority of takes come on the hang-down as the fly waves seductively in the current. One day Rob introduced me to a man who never retrieves his fly unless he's reeling in to move and who, Rob said, accounts for more fly-caught salmon than anyone else on the river. We'd see him now and then, sitting alone in the stern of his anchored rowboat as disheveled and motionless as a pile of laundry, presumably thinking private thoughts. I admired his doggedness and his record of success, but to those who don't get it, this is the sporting equivalent of watching paint dry.

Two men in a sixteen-foot drift boat are also capable of pensive silences, but eventually some conversation is inevitable. At first the old hand checks out the newcomer on the fishing and this can go on in diminishing fits and starts for days. Sooner or later, though, the talk drifts into other areas. You avoid the landmines of politics and religion unless you already know you're in complete agreement. And if you know you're in complete agreement, there's nothing much left to say. Women sometimes come up, but honesty among men on this subject is so rare that you usually just end up airing out clichés. Many of the fishermen I know have failed marriages in their pasts, and some blame the breakups on all the time and attention they spent on fishing. In fact, that may have been the precipitating event, but the real troubles usually ran deeper than they care to go into.

So you talk about work, friends, pets, boats, fishing tackle, trips to other rivers and local lore. For instance, Rob told me about a one-legged man in a wheelchair who drives up here from a nearby city in his old car and spends weeks at a time fishing from the bank. Because he doesn't have much money, he's said to back his wheelchair into the bankside brush and sleep under a tarp. Every time I start thinking I might qualify as hard core, I hear something like this and go back to feeling like a pampered tourist.

I also learned that some of the people we saw coming and going in larger boats than ours were actually part-time commercial fisher-men who sold to local restaurants that advertised "dory-caught" fish. Their schedules seemed haphazard but were strictly determined by tide, weather and their own hard-won knowledge of the fishery. On the way back from a day at sea, they might stop and pull their crab pots and then dig some clams at low tide. You wouldn't get rich at this and you'd have to supplement your income with odd jobs, but for at least part of the year you could live by your wits on the water

following an old tradition and walk around town in rubber boots looking salty and aloof.

I daydreamed about that during the next lull in the conversation.
At one time or another, I've fantasized about pulling up stakes and
moving to most of the places I've fished to make a new life, although
so far I've only done it once.

Oh yeah, and every once in a while one of us would hook a
salmon.

Rob tied the flies for this trip. That is, he brought full boxes from
home and also tied every evening in our rented cabin. An extension
cord would be stretched from the bathroom socket out to recharge
the batteries for the trolling motor, our waders and rain slickers
would be drying in front of an electric heater, and Rob would be
tying. He never seemed to hurry, but somehow trim, graceful salmon
flies on japanned black hooks accumulated at an alarming rate. Like
some other fishing guides I've known, Rob is a self-contained, slightly
compulsive bundle of energy with an eye peeled for the mundane
detail that can make all the difference. When I'd turn in at what I
thought was a reasonable hour, he'd still be up tying. When I'd get up
before dawn, he'd be rustling up breakfast or loading gear. I assume
he slept, but I can't prove it.

As time went on, I decided to keep a fish. I hadn't thought about
this beforehand, but we'd been nibbling on some salmon Rob had
smoked and it was real good. The second time I said how delicious it
was, he told me his minimalist recipe, offered to smoke one for me
and just like that I was hunting a salmon to kill. It would have to be
the brightest possible fish. A day or two earlier we'd talked to a guy
who said he'd killed a "slightly colored-up fish" and it was "not too
bad." But when you get into the area of gourmet food gathering, "not
too bad" falls short of what you have in mind.

I hooked the fish I wanted on the afternoon of our last day. We
went to the spot known as the Brush Pile for high tide and found

surprisingly few boats. I wondered if people knew something we didn't. It was chilly and raining steadily, but this hadn't struck me as a crowd that would be scared off by a little sprinkle.

Anyway, we anchored in the sweet spot and after a while I hooked a salmon. They all seem big at first, but after ten minutes this one still seemed big. He made a long downstream run, wallowed, and then swam back toward the boat with me furiously taking up slack line. Then he tried to bore into the sunken brush that gives this run its name, and I muscled him out. When we got him close enough for a look, we could see it was a dime-bright fish of about thirty pounds. He wouldn't let himself be led into the shallows but kept ducking under the boat while Rob spun it one way and then the other with the oars trying to get him into the open. We were laughing from nervousness and because even we could see that this was pretty comical.

When we finally netted him, a few people nearby in boats and on the bank hooted and clapped and then turned to speak to each other in quieter tones, saying something like, "Did you see those two clowns tryin' to land that fish?" Then we rowed to shore and killed him. He must have just come in with the tide because he still had the sea lice on him that would have fallen off after just a few hours in fresh water.

I never had second thoughts, but my happiness was leavened by the sting of regret you inevitably feel when you kill your own food instead of leaving the chore to someone else. You can't help but wonder what that light in its eyes was and where it went so suddenly. But then that quickly evolved into something less stark and more complicated—something like what Jim Harrison was getting at when he said, "Everything edible is technically dead"—and by the time Rob snapped a hero shot, I was grinning like I'd won the lottery. To some here that would all sound a little too touchy-feely, but observing the abrupt transition from beautiful live animal to piece of meat is nothing more than a way of paying attention.

I'd caught that salmon on a fly I watched Rob tie the night before. It was a pretty thing with a long tail of sparse orange bucktail barred with a black marker and topped by a few strands of tinsel, a black chenille body with an oval gold rib, soft orange hen hackle and jungle-cock sides. Why that one and none of the others, I couldn't say. It just struck me as elaborately formal, like an officer's dress uniform. Before I tied it on, I held it up and said to Rob, "Damn it, I just like the looks of this."

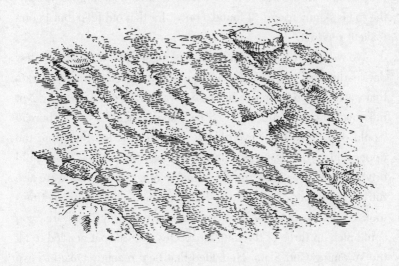

22

WYOMING

Doug and I left the last stream we fished in midmorning and drove two drainages west, making the usual stop at a crossroads general store to buy more food and fresh ice for the coolers, top off the gas tank and dispose of our accumulated camp garbage. There was a raven guarding the Dumpster from a safe distance; acting nonchalant while we emptied our trash, then gliding down when we walked away to see if we'd left him anything useful. On the way into the store, I passed too close to a parked pickup and got the evil eye from a pair of blue heelers in the bed. On the covered porch a large man was say-ing to his skinny friend, "I found a buyer for that old Jeep, but I gotta make it run first."

We were on our way to a little river a guide we'd talked to a few days earlier had told us about. He said it was a good cutthroat stream that wasn't fished too much because it was sort of out of the way. Not unknown of course, but also not the kind of place the tourist bureau would direct you to or even know about. He added that from the upper end of the drainage where the stream fished best, you could drive on over a low pass and down to two other creeks that were also full of cutthroats. This guide—Ken by name—said he sometimes took clients up there because in this one relatively small area you could pick up three of the four subspecies of cutthroat needed to fill the Wyoming Cutt Slam. He added that he'd recently talked to two guys who wanted to prove some obscure point by getting all four cut-throats in the space of twenty-four hours. He said he probably could have managed it, but begged off because, "Guidin' people in that much of a hurry didn't sound like fun."

We were on one of those trips that are left open-ended precisely to make room for this kind of mission creep, so we thought we'd check out this stream and then continue south over the pass to more cutthroat water. If nothing else, one of the creeks over there was sup-posed to hold Bonnevilles, a rare strain of cutthroat neither of us had ever knowingly caught.

Ken's directions matched the map, and we easily found the stream and the dirt road that followed it up a narrow, unpopulated valley. This was an ordinary little watershed with no snow-capped peaks suitable for real estate with expensive views and slopes too low for a ski area. There'd been some firewood cutting but no logging, some open-range grazing but no signs of actual ranching. The work that was done here over the years had been marginal and low-paying, and like much of the West, the place now had that used and abandoned look that made it seem more feral than truly wild. At uneven intervals we crossed small tributaries with names like Blind Mule Creek and Dead Horse Creek that recalled those older, harder times.

This was a gentle valley with a low but steady gradient, and the stream was a uniform riffle lacking the obvious pools, plunges and glides of recognizable trout water. It didn't look all that inviting—or at least didn't look like a photo from a daydream-inducing coffee table book—so we drove on up the road at a speed that made the ticking of gravel in the wheel wells sound like corn popping. It was a warm, windless summer day. We had the windows down and a plume of dust hung behind us like a wake. It was fifty miles to the pass. If we saw water we wanted to fish, we'd stop. Otherwise we'd go on over the top and look at the creeks on the other side. We were four days, two streams and dozens of trout into the trip; intoxicated by movement and comfortable in the faith that farther up the road there'd be something better.

At about the forty-mile mark, we came to a Forest Service sign saying that the two bridges up ahead were under repair and the pass was closed. "Shit," Doug said. "Why didn't they tell us that down at the mouth of the valley?"

Well, probably because this was a hundred and some miles of dirt road that went nowhere in particular except south and didn't see a lot of through traffic. Since we left pavement, we'd seen exactly one other vehicle: a pickup with another pair of blue heelers in back. When we passed on the narrow road, the dogs barked at us ferociously as the driver touched a finger to the bill of his cap in a neighborly way.

By this time we'd decided that the stream we'd been following could qualify as the longest continuous riffle in North America and we didn't much like the looks of it. It was said to hold the original Snake River cutthroats that were indigenous to the drainage, but with no apparent holding water, we thought it could only support a struggling population of small native fish. That might account for the lack of traffic and the fact that we hadn't seen a single fisherman in forty miles.

Doug pulled in at the first two-track we came to and parked in a grove of spruce trees along the stream. The slope had been gradual, but we'd slowly passed from a cottonwood and juniper bottom into open coniferous woods where the air had the tang of altitude. This was the point you inevitably reach on an aimless trip that's either a dead end or the cusp of a breakthrough: time to stop, get out of the truck and think things over.

But of course this wasn't a complicated equation. We couldn't get over the pass and it was too late in the day to turn back. We'd stopped at a place that would do well enough for a quick overnight, so we decided we'd work out our next move in the morning. In the meantime, we had two hours of daylight left and decided we might as well spend half of it fishing before we came back and pitched camp.

Working out where to put a dry fly in what appears to be a bank-to-bank riffle is an exercise in attentiveness. It all looks more or less the same at first, but only because you're not looking closely enough. So you make a few tentative casts, testing the drift and the speed of the current, which is invariably either faster or slower than it looks. You're warming up, idly dribbling the ball while you wait for the juju to kick in. There may or may not be any trout in here, but if there are, you know they'll be tucked in whatever dead water they can find, waiting to dart into the current to grab passing insects. Riffles aren't typically good holding or wintering water, but they *are* the oxygen-dissolving, insect-generating engine of any trout stream. If nothing else, this thing amounted to a fifty-mile-long bug factory.

So your dry fly bobs along at speed on what appears to be a monotonous washboard surface, only to stall momentarily in minia-ture slicks or pressure waves. Sometimes you're still in the process of registering that this has happened when the fly simply vanishes.

Maybe it went down in a rise that was indistinguishable from all the other moving bumps of current, or maybe it was sucked under by errant drag on your leader. The early-evening light is simultaneously dull and shiny, so it's hard to be sure, but the fly you're watching is suddenly not there and you instinctively tighten up.

My first trout seemed to come out of nowhere. It was an eight-inch cutthroat: nothing to write home about, but a fish nonetheless and a well-fed, muscular little guy at that. When I cradled him in the water to remove the hook, he felt as round, hard and slick as a brat-wurst covered in wet silk.

My second fish *didn't* seem to come out of nowhere. I was bearing down now, with that sense familiar to fishermen that tomorrow may be another day, but in the present time and place, this is your only chance to get it right. I was picking out the spots where the current seemed to suggest divots in the bottom large enough to shelter a trout, and after a dozen more casts my fly was quietly sucked into one. It was another fat eight-incher and I wondered if this is what Ken had meant. If so, I couldn't argue. As a small-stream fisherman with modest expectations and a weakness for wild cutthroats, I might also describe a mountain creek full of fat eight-inchers as "good."

Doug passed me on the bank heading upstream and we compared notes. He'd done about the same—a couple of small trout—but he was into it now, too, and so didn't stop to chat.

A little farther on I cast to the kind of spot you could miss from any distance in the confusion of chop, but up close I could see a boil of current indicating a bigger submerged rock. Behind it was a jumpy slick large enough to hold a football, and when I put a cast over this, I saw the head and shoulders of a trout roll downstream as he took the fly. The motion was mercurial in the low, chromy light, but there was unmistakable life and purpose in it.

I set up on a heavier fish that pulled the slack line from my left hand and then took more off the reel as it ran down and across the current. I'd been so convinced that there wouldn't be any big fish in here that for a second I wondered if I'd foul-hooked an otter, but I was walking it downstream and playing it back to my side of the creek and there was just no way this wasn't a trout. By the time I landed it, Doug was standing beside me. I don't remember if I called to him or if he just saw the bend in the rod and came down to see what I had.

It was a beautiful cutthroat no less than sixteen inches long and so deep-bodied I couldn't get my hand around it. Doug said, "Well look at that."

We fished late and didn't get camp set up before dark, so we ended up doing the last few chores by the uncertain light of head-lamps. Finding a place to pitch your tent is more time-consuming than tossing your duffel on the bed in a hotel room. At a bare mini-mum, you want a level patch with no rocks or exposed roots that's in soil soft enough to sink a tent peg and that's not under any of the leaning dead trees loggers call "widow makers." But beyond that there's also some seemingly pointless pacing and circling reminiscent of a dog looking for a place to lie down. As any golden retriever could tell you, you're not after perfection, just the kind of down-home feng shui that avoids disharmony.

By the time we were fed and watching the fire from folding chairs, the air had turned cold and the sky was full of stars. It was only then that I settled into the relief every traveler feels at having temporarily lit somewhere.

The next morning was clear and frosty, and we lingered over breakfast and a second pot of coffee until the day's busyness began among the pine squirrels, chickadees and caddis flies. When things seemed right, we got in where we'd left off the night before and waded upstream in ankle-deep water, flicking short, busy casts. In morning sun the clear water was a moving window. Strictly speak-ing, the stream was still a continuous riffle, but I could now see tubs, channels and potholes that stood out clearly where the rocky bottom went from mottled grayish brown to the faint olive cast that betrays depth. I'd spot the color first and only then notice the corrugated nervousness of the current where it stalled into what passed for holding water. On a cast with the right upstream mend, a dry fly would dance down into this bumpy slick and seem to downshift. A second or two later, as often as not, a nice cutthroat would roll on it in an unhurried, businesslike way and I'd come up tight, still surprised after all these years at the sudden live weight of a fish.

We worked upstream at a good clip. There were long stretches of shallow, fishless water—calf-deep, fast and wobbly with loose cobbles—but we stayed in the river for fear of missing even one little slick where a trout might be hiding. The biggest fish were lying in the best-looking spots as if this were an illustration in a book by an expert fisherman. I was feeling like a pretty handy sport, not only catching trout, but wading past the barren water and calling my shots: skipper behind that little rock; fat fifteen-incher at the head of that slick. Unexamined happiness is the purest kind, but it didn't sully the experience to think that although there are plenty of things I'd change about my life given the chance, this wasn't one of them. During a break for lunch Doug and I admitted that we were both embarrassed at having almost driven right by all this and grateful for the dumb luck that had made us stop.

I'm not saying where this stream was for the usual obvious reasons, but I *will* say that the great state of Wyoming has more than its fair share of these small, surprisingly good trout streams that fall outside the boundaries of efficient itineraries and are therefore largely ignored or overlooked. This is the predictable result of 97,812 square miles with a population roughly one sixth that of Denver and with the pressure from visiting fishermen concentrated along well-worn tourist routes where hospitality is a profession. It's not that the folks out in the countryside are standoffish, but a friend once said that every time I go to Wyoming the population of liberals temporarily doubles and that doesn't always go unnoticed. But then I go there to fish, not to discuss politics.

We fished for two days, covering a sweet spot that stretched five miles upstream from camp and ended abruptly where a tributary emptied into a good run. This is where Doug landed two trout as perfectly matched as bookends, both about eighteen inches long. These were the two biggest cutthroats we landed, but there had been some others that came close. Above that confluence pool, both forks were too small to be much more than nursery water, but we waded up both just to make sure. At the highest point I heard a distant piping sound that might have been an unfamiliar bird or the backup horn on a bulldozer working on the bridges upstream. I stopped to listen but lost it in the white nose of running water.

We broke camp that afternoon, determined to find a route that would take us on south toward those Bonneville cutthroats without going all the way back the way we came. We backtracked a few miles down the drainage and turned east along a little feeder called Sheep Creek. By staying on what seemed to be the most heavily traveled road, we threaded our way up a narrow, one-lane pass and then gradually down the other side, out of the cool spruce and pine through descending foothills and onto a high sage bench. We weren't entirely sure where we were, but we had half a tank of gas and were tending generally in the right direction on an unmarked but serviceable dirt road that was bound to lead somewhere sooner or later.

The first vehicle we saw was a pickup going in the opposite direction and the driver flagged us down and asked for directions. We said we thought we were still on a certain-numbered Forest Service road, but that we'd passed enough unmarked and unmapped forks that we couldn't actually swear to it. I'd been studying the map while Doug drove, so I went on to say that the watercourse along the road was probably South Cottonwood Creek, although it could be *North* Cottonwood or, if we'd strayed farther south than I thought, maybe

Apperson or even North Piney. Once I said this out loud, it didn't sound as helpful as I'd intended.

We were stopped side by side blocking the road in the fashion of rural Wyoming with the compass and map spread out on the guy's hood. His wife and young daughter were still sitting in the cab acting either patient or bored—it was hard to tell—but his dog, a large brown mutt with a hint of pit bull, had jumped out of the open pickup bed and was doing his best to scare up a rabbit.

I pointed to where I thought we were on the map. The guy nodded thoughtfully and pointed at a different spot where *he* thought we were. That seemed to settle it for both of us. He whistled up his dog and we parted amiably, agreeing that one or the other of us was lost.

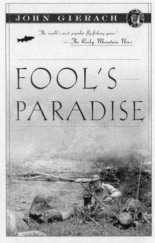
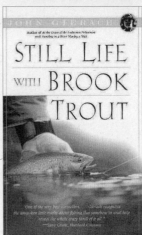